ETERNAL INDIA

Bodhisatva Padmapani, Son of Buddha Amitabha. A twenty-inch Nepalese bronze owned by the author

ALFRED NAWRATH

ETERNAL INDIA

THE LAND, THE PEOPLE,

THE MASTERPIECES OF ARCHITECTURE

AND SCULPTURE

OF INDIA, PAKISTAN, BURMA AND CEYLON

ILLUSTRATED WITH

106 BLACK-AND-WHITE AND 12 FULL-COLOR

PHOTOGRAPHS TAKEN BY THE AUTHOR

CROWN PUBLISHERS, INC., NEW YORK

In memory of my mother,
who in 1953 has gone home to her eternity

Library of Congress Catalog Card Number, 56–11367
Prepared in collaboration with Chanticleer Press, Inc., New York
Printed by Christoph Reisser's Söhne, Vienna, Austria

PREFACE

The poet, the scholar, or the artist who launches a book into the world is like a man entrusting his offering to a river. He does not know which shores it will reach, into whose hands it will fall. He hopes the receiver will be worthy; but maybe unworthy ones will fish it out, or perhaps it will disappear completely in the whirling waters.

If it is conceivable that the author worries over the fate of his mind's offspring, how much more are the bookseller and the collector entitled to misgivings on their part. Countless are the new art books published each year. Many are topical, dependent on economic conditions or lacking in subject matter—like the creations, or rather the products, of a vogue in painting.

Five extensive journeys that extended over a period of several years were necessary to shape the pictorial material and collect the knowledge on which this book is based. A merciful providence has kept my youthful enthusiasm alive and robbed me of little of my physical powers, despite the fact that I am nearing life's exit. Knowing that the type for this book was being set and that all was in good hands in Vienna, at the beginning of last September I embarked once again for India.

The spiritual heritage of thousands of years is seen in the plates of this book. All the monuments speak their own unmistakable language which I have prudently refrained from endeavoring to interpret—conscious of the inadequacy of my words.

Should I have succeeded in awakening a feeling of friendship among those living outside the confines of India for that great and highly cultured nation that has given an imperishable contribution to the development of mankind, then I should feel myself amply rewarded for the privations and hardships entailed by travel in its remotest regions.

Easter Sunday, 1956   E. A. Nawrath

INTRODUCTION AND COMMENTARY TO THE PLATES

BURMA

It is June 17, 1954. The Greek tramp steamer, based on the island of Hydra, taking me on to Indonesia, has a hard battle with the racing, muddy current of the lower Irrawaddy. For several days the south-westerly monsoon has covered the country with flood-like torrents of water. Ten years have elapsed since the end of World War II, but the pier of Rangoon still stands in ruins, destroyed by the bombs that Japanese planes discharged on the British, and British on the Japanese in the alternating struggle for Burma. This is a land rich in rice, teak, petroleum, and the key to one of the most important gateways to Central Asia.

On a hill above the town glitters Shwe Dagon, Rangoon's Golden Pagoda (Plate 1). In the dreadful nights of bombing and burning its broad terraces offered shelter to tens of thousands. The so-called "Christian" Nations destroyed each other's cathedrals, but the Japanese did not violate this shrine of their Buddhist brothers.

Out of the original form of the earth-heaped Tumulus developed the early Buddhist Stupa, which is still most clearly distinguishable in Sanchi (Plate 8). Gradually the Stupa became the massive circular pagoda, shown in Plate 6. To lend it greater dignity, it was raised on to a profiled square or polygonal base and finally, it was given its slender, uplifting bell shape so that it might soar up more loftily into the clear blue of the skies. The standard shape for the Burmese pagoda had been found.

The pagoda is no communal meeting place like the synagogue, the Christian church or the Mohammedan mosque; it is solely a reminder and reliquary. Because of the strong tapering of the pagoda, which is coated with 25 tons of pure gold, the visitor is not aware that the enormous building is 364 feet high excluding the umbrella-shaped, bejewelled Ti, whose golden and silver bells tinkle gently and melodiously in the slightest breeze.

Red laquered, richly gilded chapels, the votive offerings of devout pilgrims, huddle around the titanic main building seeking protection like chickens under their mother's wing. Between the inner and the larger concentric outer circle of chapels runs a marble-panelled promenade, which at night is festively illuminated and which can justly claim to be the most magnificent, the most international, and the most sacred of its kind in the world. As the Moslems from Marocco to the Moluccas, from Serajevo to Khartoum, meet together in Mecca, so pilgrims from all parts of the Buddhist world gather here. They come from Burma and Ceylon, from Thailand, Cambodja and Korea, from Japan and the immense land of China. Their homelands represent half the world's population. He who looks at the globe from Washington invariably sees only the one, perhaps even the less promising of the two halves of the globe. Here is the other half.

The large paddle steamer that once travelled from Rangoon right up to the Chinese frontier (a total distance of 1,000 miles) has covered six hundred miles. Twice it has run aground, despite careful sounding, and the sun is setting as we near Pagan. For twenty miles we are accompanied by ruins and pagodas. As they rise up on the left bank of the river, we think of another sun setting behind the flowing red tamarisks, far away beyond the sea: Buddha's teaching had returned to the bosom of Brahmanism, where it had originated. No bloody "heresy" persecution had extirpated it from its original home—spiritual warfare by force of arms remained a privilege of the Western world. Buddhism had to give place to intellectual forces that sprang to life within Brahmanism, opened by great poet-philosophers like Shankara—a contemporary of Charlemagne. The ancient gods of India were powerful again—each of the stone reliefs in Ellora (Plates 77—82) joyfully proclaims this fact. Mysticism had triumphed over pure doctrine, which was as relentless as the ethical demands of Kant. Islam was penetrating from the West. Its doctrine, too, possessed a powerful appeal; it knew no caste barriers, but embraced all, without distinction of education and property. In this time of extremity, the doctrine of "the Exalted One," "the completely Enlightened One," which continued to flourish in Ceylon, thanks to royal patronage, found a new protector on the mainland, who in religious zeal was not inferior to Asoka himself. This was Anawrata—a contemporary of Henry IV and Henry's great opponent, Pope Gregory—the first truly great king of Burma, who unified the country, made it a refuge of Buddhism and opened the way for Buddhism in all the lands of India. A great number of monks with shaven heads and yellow togas came from India, bringing the sacred books with them, and instructed the youth in the doctrine of the Master—as they are still wont to do today: "Even were a man to carry his mother on one shoulder and his father on the other, and were he to live thus for a hundred years, he would still not have shown them sufficient gratitude and repaid them for their kindness ... If a man is overtaken by Death and must leave his earthly life, what remains to him and what accompanies him hence—who follows him and does not part from him? Two things, the good and the bad that a mortal has done on earth remain with him—they accompany him from hence, and follow after him like a shadow that never leaves him. Therefore man should do that which is good" (cf. Winternitz).

I am standing in the 900-year-old pagoda built by King Kyanzittha. It is dedicated to Ananda, the disciple "whom the Master loved." Stone reliefs comprehensible to the ordinary man who cannot read the Jatakas clearly and impressively depict the legends of the Buddha's previous existences. Through a narrow opening in the ceiling a magical light falls on the giant, thirty-foot-high golden statue of the Master, who has his right hand raised, teaching and blessing: "May all creatures live in peace and happiness, may all have joy in their hearts. Be they visible or invisible, far or near, already born or still awaiting birth—may all beings be joyful in their hearts!" Twilight falls and they blend into one: the consecrating Buddha and Thorwaldsen's consecrating Christ. All is quiet in the darkening pagoda. Gentle voices come to my ear, as if from very far

away. Stray tones from the Sermon on the Mount? Little Burmese girls with delicate, garlanded hair styles and flowered silk dresses pray softly, the small hands folded over the forehead; then they place a tiny doll's bowl of rice before the image of the divine Teacher. Through the narrow opening in the ceiling above the head of the statue fall the gentle rays of daylight. The gilded mouth smiles kindly; the Exalted One thanks innocence for its offering.

The town grew rapidly and soon became the nursery of Buddhist learning. The library, whose roof is reminiscent of China, was built about the same time as the Ananda pagoda. Ever more splendid pagodas sprang up—magnificent terraced buildings with chapels at the corners: Thatbyinnyu, "the Omniscient" (Plate 2), Gawdawpalin, "the Ancestral Throne" and the proud Maha Bodhi (Plate 3) that leads to the Master's northern Indian homeland. Then came Kubla Khan to take revenge on King Nara-thi-ha-pati for the murder of a Chinese diplomatic delegation. He was accompanied by millions of warriors. Why should we doubt that number? We should also be inclined to doubt that Pagan contained 13,000 pagodas and monasteries, yet archeologists who have measured the area of the town declare that it was 100 square miles and they have topographically proved the existence of 5,000 pagodas. In order to defend the town, thousands of pagodas were pulled down so that the tiles could be used to strengthen the ramparts. The golden age of Pagan lasted only two and a half centuries—a short period, for Asia counts in millenniums. The enigmatic town on the Irrawaddy rose and fell like a meteor.

It is another hundred miles by river to Mandalay, the last capital of Burma before its conquest by the English. Large vessels glide past us, some as richly carved as the boats of kings. From the banks innumerable pagodas greet us, erected by the devout, mostly bell-shaped, rising straight up from the ground. The rampart behind which the palace is hidden is bloodred. The latter was built only in 1857, the same year that the insurrection broke out in India. However, it remains true to tradition. Similar to it must have been the wooden palisaded palace of Chandragupta, at whose court in Pataliputra (Patna) Megasthenes the Greek resided as the ambassador from King Seleukos Nikator. The roomy palace with its dark-red lacquered, wooden pillars, its richly

8

carved and gilded thrones, its open garden halls, clearly shows the influence of neighboring China, whose army invaded Burma at the time of Kubla Khan and sacked Pagan in 1287.

The excellence of Mindon Min, who built the palace, both as a man and a ruler was matched in infamy by the royal couple that succeeded him on the throne of the Lion and the Lily. While conducting a love affair with the depraved Supaya Lat, the young weak-willed Prince Thibaw came under the influence of her ambitious mother, Alenan-daw, the Queen of the Middle Palace, and seized the throne while Mindon Min still lay on his deathbed (1878). The first act of his reign was to murder his brothers and sisters in the most bestial fashion. Disgusted, the British ambassador left the Royal court. On November 14, 1885, Indian troops crossed the Burmese frontier, and on the 29th the last Burmese royal couple was escorted into exile in India, where Thibaw died, inglorious and forgotten, at the end of 1916.

A gong is struck; Pungis come. "Shaven heads, eyes lowered, carrying the alms bowl under the long toga, the monk accepts what is given; he waits for that which is given him with a purified heart. Once a day he will eat, but far be it from him to eat at the wrong time. By eating once a day he retains health and vigor, vigilance, strength and well-being." Emphatically the Master warns against the "danger of the Crocodile (Greed)": "What the monk has heard here, he will not repeat there so as to cause a quarrel there, and what he hears over there, he will not repeat here, so as to cause discord. Thus he unites those at variance, strengthens allies; concord makes him glad." Without looking up, they receive their rice: "It is not meet for a monk to look at the gifts he is given." No word of thanks crosses their lips: "Does the earth thank the cloud for rain?" Deep in thought I gaze after them. Would that I could remain longer among you—in Buddha's favorite land!

Pegu (Plate 4)

The ancient capital of the Talaings was founded in 573 by two brothers named Thamala and Wimala. Later the younger slew the elder. The story of its foundation has a remarkable similarity to that of the founding of Rome. After a period of decline the town, which at that time was still situated on the sea coast, experienced a new prosperity in the six-teenth century. In 1519 its king signed a trade agreement with Portugal. About the middle of the century the power of the trading city extended as far as Thailand. Even if the report of the Venetian, Cesar Frederick—that twenty-five crowned rulers owed allegiance to the king, that in his service he had one-and-a-half million warriors and four thousand elephants which could be caught at the very gates of the capital—even if this report cannot be taken quite literally, Pegu under Branginoco (Bayin Naung, 1551—1581), was certainly an equal partner to the city of lagoons. Frederick praised especially the honesty of her ruby traders. The image of the Buddha (Shwethalyaung) with its Mongolian-shaped eyes, 180 feet long and 45 feet high at the shoulders, which was discovered in 1881 as railroads were being laid through the jungle, is the most convincing proof of former greatness. The monument was erected in 994 by Migadeikpa Min-ngè. It was lost when Alompra (Alaungpaya) conquered and laid waste the city in 1757.

Pagan (Plates 2, 3)

"As countless as the pagodas of Pagan" runs an old Burmese saying. The ruins extend for a distance of twenty miles along the waterfront, ranging five miles inland! Nothing remains of the royal palaces and the common people's huts that were probably built of straw matting, as they still are today. Only the temples tower proudly. They do not rise bell-shaped from the ground as do the more modest buildings of today, but are enthroned on a lofty and massive stone base, out of which narrow galleries and small shrines for the images of the Buddha have been hollowed. The roofs are invariably pyramidal, gradated several times. The terraces, intended for processional purposes, are flanked by small corner towers. The outline is usually square, though the Ananda pagoda has the form of a Greek cross. The Thatbyinnyu, built about 1100 by Kyanzittha's grandson, measures almost six hundred square feet and is two hundred feet high. Tiles were used throughout as building material. The sculptured ornamentation always remains subordinate to the complete outer form and is executed in stucco.

Mandalay (Plate 7)

Just as the Irrawaddy is a single, clear and transparent stream while it flows through the mountains but grows more turbid the farther it gets from its source until when it finally reaches the Delta it is completely silted up and sand-clogged, so the Buddhist doctrine gradually became shallower, clouded by side-streams the farther it became removed in time from the Master. King Mindon Min summoned a scholarly Council that after three years' work established a critical edition of the Tipitaka. The authentic text was engraved on 729 man-high marble tablets, which are preserved for posterity in 729 small chapels, surrounding a main building 98 feet high, similar to the stone panels in the Confucius temple in Peking. Our picture shows the Queens Golden Monastery. Mighty stairs, flanked by wide, projecting stone volutes lead up to the terraced building, with its opulent carrings and its ornamental galleries. The sun and the tropical rains have seriously damaged the gilded teakwood, but even nowadays, scholarly monks with their novices live in the secluded ruins, endeavoring to keep the sacred scriptures alive and to exorcise the curse that is associated with the name of the founder.

Amarapura (Plate 5)

As in ancient Egypt, so did the capitals change in Burma: Amarapura was founded in 1783 by Bawdawpaya, the fifth son of Alompra, who began his reign by burning alive all his brothers, together with their wives and children. When shortly thereafter, Mindon Min transferred his court to Mandalay, six miles to the North of Amarapura, his primary reason was most probably to escape the frightful memories associated with "the Immortal One," as Bawdawpaya had called the town. The King, a victim of Caesarean madness, had ambitions to erect a pagoda 488 feet high, which was to be the highest in the Buddhist world. The building, which was to be square, measured 455 feet in length and breadth and had attained a third of its projected height when an oracle discouraged the king from fulfilling his purpose. The gigantic base, shaken by an earthquake in 1838, still towers aloft at Mingun, and beside it stands the great 87-ton bell—the largest ringing one in the world.

One is struck by the many Chinese features among the population, distant descendants of Kublai Khan's warriors. The art of silk weaving is highly developed. Also the Dragon pagoda indicates Chinese influence. Another pagoda is completely covered by tiny images of the Buddha, set in small niches. Whereas the Singhalese seated Buddha is always portrayed with both hands clasped together, the Burmese Buddha rests his right hand on his knee, with the fingers, all of equal length, pointing downwards.

Sagaing (Plate 6)

The town was founded six and a half centuries ago, after the destruction of Pagan. In front of the Kaunghmudaw rise giant griffons which also flank the bottom of the steep stairways leading from the river up to the hillside pagodas. (Since 1934 a nine-arched road-and-railway bridge over a mile long crosses the river at Sagaing, whose foundations had to be laid 126 feet below the low-water mark because of the trencherous ground and the tremendous flow of the water.)

CEYLON

1840 wide steps lead up to the heights of Mihintale (Plate 8). Looking out upon the forests, from which the lakes sparkle like bright eyes, they sat there together more than 2000 years ago. Tissa, King of Ceylon, wanted to hunt the stag, but he brought home something more precious from this mountain top. The great Asoka's equally great son, the royal monk from Magadha, had come hither through the air, filled with the same apostalic zeal as his father, to spread the divine message. In socratic dialogue, he tested the king and found him wise, worthy to comprehend the exalted doctrine of love, charity, and infinite compassion which Gautama, the Muni (Seer) from the land of the Sakker had preached two hundred years earlier: Buddha, "the Lord, the Holy One, the completely Enlightened One, perfect in knowledge and conduct, the Blessed One, judge of worlds, teacher of the gods and men." The birds interrupted their flight and listened as they later listened to St. Francis of Assisi. Clearly Mahinda's words come to us over the space of two thousand years: He tells of the Buddha's childhood whose very birth brought a glorious splendor into the world. We hear how at twenty-nine he fled from domestic happiness, throwing off all earthly ties in order to overcome human suffering through the power of intellect and will. "With him, the Exalted One seeks refuge, in whom I have found my refuge." And the royal messenger succeeded in planting "the roots of goodness" in the king's heart. Later the great Asoka's equally great son Mahinda found his last resting-place on this same hill which was named after him. A palm-sheltered pagoda guards his tomb. But more impressive than the pagoda is the solemn jungle landscape that witnessed the event.

In order to prove (outwardly) the Singhalese adherents of Buddhism to be true offshoots of the original community of Buddhists, Dewanampia Tissa, "the friend of the gods," begged for a twig of the tree of enlightenment. Sanghamitta, Mahinda's sister, brought it in person to Lanka; the eighteenth and nineteenth chapters of the ancient Singhalese chronicles of Kings give detailed reports of the event: In the presence of the "Ruler of the Earth" (Asoka) a twig of the Bodhi-tree transplanted itself into a golden vase, at which the whole universe lit up and "men's hearts opened up like the lotus blossom on the pond beneath the rays of the sun." The journey down the Ganges lasted seven days to the harbor; the sea voyage another seven. Eight golden and eight silver ornamented ships escorted them. As soon as King Tissa caught sight of the fleet he was the first to go to meet them, wading in the water up to his neck, and he bore the holy twig ashore in his own hands. When it was planted the earth quaked, elephants trumpeted for joy. Then rain clouds descended from the skies and hid the twig for seven days until it had taken root in Singhalese earth, "Mahamegha's delightful garden." The tree still flourishes in Tissa's ancient capital, Anuradhapura!

Tissa reigned for 40 years, from 236—276 of the Buddhist era (307—267 B. C. according to the most probable calculations). Two generations later came the "damilos." The Tamil prince Elala from Chola-land (southern India) made himself king. He too ruled wisely (205—161 B.C.). Everyone was permitted to enter the palace; even when the king was asleep the suppliant could ring a bell that was suspended over the king's bed. Once a cow pulled at the bellrope "in the bitterness of her heart" because the king's son had carelessly killed her calf. And Elala's son had to expiate the crime by his own death. Elala lost his throne to Dutugemunu, who has remained the national hero of the Singhalese right up to modern times.

In reading the twenty-fifth chapter of the Chronicles of Kings, one actually relives the struggle for Elala's throne. Dutugemunu's war elephant, Kandula, charged with his mighty head against the iron-plated gates of the fortress. The enemy poured white-hot iron balls and boiling pitch down upon him. He trotted to a nearby pond to cool his wounds, then rammed the gate with renewed fury until he wrenched it from its hinges and trampled them down. At the South gate of Anuradhapura, mentioned by Ptolemy as Anurogrammum Regia, Elala prepared for chivalrous single combat. Both kings were mounted on riding elephants. Elala fell. Dutugemunu—"he was worthy of the title of king"—buried his adversary with full martial honors and raised a mighty funeral mound to him, which even today commands awe and respect.

Dutugemunu's reign lasted only a quarter of a century, yet it was the happiest era of the "Lion's Island" up to the time of the great Parakrama Bahu. Sixteen hundred granite pillars, each thirteen feet high, of which the majority are still standing, supported the nine-story, copper-plated wooden palace, whose glitter provided its name, Lohapasada, "brazen palace." Because the inner quadrangular pillars are bulkier than the outer, we must imagine a terraced building similar to the only four-story, stone mausoleum of the Emperor Akbar in Sikandra. The twenty-seventh chapter of the Mahawansa gives a detailed account of its past splendor. The royal throne was of ivory with a seat of crystal; on the back was an imitation firmament: the sun in gold, the moon in silver, the stars in pearls. The old Pali —the chronicle which Mahanama the scholarly monk began to write in the fifth century A.D. at the time when the Chinese scholar Fa-Hsien was travelling through Ceylon—mentions that the workers actually received wages—rice and milk, ghi (refined buffalo butter), honey, and sugar.

The great king's masterpiece was the Ruanweli Dagoba (Mahathupa). No fewer than four chapters of the Mahawansa are devoted to its construction. Strong elephants, their feet reinforced by leather pads, stamped the tile foundation. Then the king himself laid the foundation stone. The reliquary contained an imitation of the Bodhi tree. Its roots were coral, bedded in sapphires; the trunk was of silver. A circle of four hundred stone elephants, heads facing out, supported the circular edifice (Plate 77). Their tusks were real ivory.

The king's dying glance rested on the Ruanweli. Since then forest has reconquered the territory that human hands wrung from it two thousand years ago. Now deep in the jungle there dreams a stone effigy of the Buddha, body erect, the eyes lowered and half closed in absorbed meditation listening to the voice from within.

In amusing fashion they trot along one behind the other(Plate 17): the elephant with curled-up trunk, the humpbacked oxen, the horse and the lion (whose likeness is not quite accurate as the mason had probably never seen a live one). An undulating frieze is followed by a herd of sacred geese carrying lotus blossoms in their beaks, and in the middle shines half a lotus bloom. One frequently comes across the lotus flower in pictures of the Master who was often portrayed enthroned on a lotus bud. Indeed, the lotus flower became the sacred emblem of Buddhism. As the blue, the red or the white lotus blossom remains pure and unsullied amidst the slimey pond, so shall man keep himself pure and unsullied in the sinful world that surrounds him and has given him birth. The four beasts in Polonnaruwa are probably symbolic of the four points of the compass. They are separated into four different friezes, whereby the number of figures and concentric bands is increased but beauty and unity are sacrificed.

The custom of entering sacred places barefoot has preserved the bas-relief so wonderfully that it stretches out in front of the stairs like a precious carpet. The steps are supported by slightly caricatured, cowering dwarfs with bullet tummies and are richly ornamented. Here again the masons of Polonnaruwa overdid things (Plate 9). The builder of Anuradhapura used them sparingly—only at the corners and in the middle of the steps.

We climb up the vertical wall on iron ladders protected from behind by iron netting in case someone should suddenly suffer from dizziness (Plate 14). Not a soul anywhere; as far as the eye can see there stretches nothing but the silent, blue-green jungle. However, on the walls of the grotto, we are surprised by attractive women (Plates 15, 16). They wear flowers, fruit and heavy, costly ornaments—

mistress and servant, both so resplendent that it is impossible to distinguish one from the other. The voluptuous figures (Plates 73, 74), the rich, unbroken colors have suffered little considering that the Sigiriyan frescos were exposed to the open air for one and a half thousand years.

Not far from Aukana, where a forty-two-feet high Buddha carved out of the live rock in the twelfth century towers alone in the jungle, lies a lake, the Kalawewa. King Dhatu Sena had it made to render the land more fertile. His son, Kasyapa was vexed by his father's large expenditure and one day demanded to know where all his treasures lay. The aged Dhatu Sena asked to be taken to the lake and pointing to the dammed-up water and to the learned monk Mahanama who accompanied him, said, "These are the only treasures that I possess." Whereupon Kasyapa had him emtombed alive. Fearing the vengeance of his brother Mogallana the paricide left the capital, Anuradhapura, and built himself a refuge on this rock, daily on the lookout for armed men on the horizon coming to avenge Dhatu Sena. He remained up there for eigtheen years; then faced his brother in open battle. Kasyapa was defeated and ended his infamous life by cutting his own throat. Ever since, the place has been accursed. Even the beasts of the jungle avoid it. Only wild bees swarm round us. The beautiful women of Sigiriya smile sensually, and the jungle guards its secret.

Cathedrals, lofty and light like those built by Cistercians in the jungle, have the tranquility of my Silesian homeland. In the apse are huge effigies of the Buddha, who had long since become a god. Luxuriant, tangled roots of tropical creeper had cracked the walls but also held them together until the English explorers arrived. They checked further decay and commendably repaired and restored the sacred memorials of the Buddhists. England is tolerant towards those of different faith and thought, just as that Buddhist king who erected a special temple in his capital, Palonnaruwa, "for the reconciliatory practice of the Brahman rites."

At the time of the great Parakrama Bahu, Polonnaruwa had fourteen gates. We still have their names: The King's, the Lion's, the Elephant's, the Snake's, the Water Gate, etc. Twenty-nine chapters of the Mahawansa are devoted to the King Parakrama, a contemporary of Barbarossa and one of the wisest rulers ever to have reigned. He gave his ministers strict instructions "never to leave a plot of land untilled, however small it may be." Neither was the slightest amount of rainfall permitted to flow into the sea without having served some useful purpose to mankind. The king knew how to fill the State treasury without oppressing his people. Everywhere he saw to it in person that justice was done; true of Hadrian before him and Frederick the Great after him: "He visited the sick and gave them their medicine with his own hands ... Before his resplendent beauty the loveliness of Spring melted into a shadow and the beautiful women of the town shed tears of joy at the sight of him." Perhaps it is the king who turned to stone and lies dreaming deep in the heart of the jungle, like Barbarossa in the heart of the Kyffhäuser mountain, an aged, bearded, twice life-sized man reading with half-closed eyes an ola (palm-leaf scroll). The statue has been interpreted as that of a religious teacher from southern India. The fez-like headdress and the odd, drooping moustache do indeed give an outlandish impression. Nevertheless, it is in no way improbable that the pious king had himself portrayed in the attitude of a sage.

We take our leave, respectfully bowing before H. M. Kalinga Chakrawarti Parakrama Bahu, who "banished poverty, transformed the island of Lanka into an island of joy, and made it like a tree of good fortune."

A mile away, deep in the primeval forest, rests a sleeper (Plate 10). His hair is delicately curled as befits a king's son; the robe finely pleated, as if damply pressed. The figure which it emphasizes rather than hides is that of a completely flawless man. The Lord Gautama, in whose veins flowed mountain blood—for his home, Kapilavastu, adjoins Nepal—was favored with all the thirty-two attributes of a great man. "Such a one can follow only two courses; no third is possible. If he remains at home he will become king, a true and just ruler, a victor right up to the sea and bring security to this land. If he leaves home and wanders homeless, he will become holy, omniscient and will unveil the secrets of the world." The Lord Gautama, as we call him by the name of a Vedic seer, was destined to become the leader of an army, according to his father's wishes (his mother died seven days after his birth). And the Lord Gautama did indeed become the leader of a host. Now he rests from his journeying; a deep dreamless sleep has sunk upon the lids of him that is released from all pain. "Life has been drained, the work is done, the way that brings insight and knowledge found." The trees of the jungle rustle mysteriously, as then, when the octogenarian entered Nirvana in the mango grove by Cunda the Smith's: "At that moment, although it was not flowering time, all the fallow trees burst into glorious blossom. The blossoms scattered covering the body of the Tathagata over and over again to do him honor. And heavenly sandalwood dust fell from the air and harps sounded in the breezes to do honor to the Tathagata." Sorrowfully at his head stands Ananda, "he who expects the sublime, who is near the sublime." Even today deep perplexity is revealed in his expression, though the heavy monsoon rains have streamed down that face for centuries. Yet the dying Master comforted the weeping one: "You have the laws that I have found. You have my teachings, and in them I shall always be with you. Do not forget that life and death are one. Never forget that. For I have gathered you together for that purpose. Life and death are one."

Singhalese monks wrote down the words in Pali that the sacred mouth uttered in the popular dialect of the land of Magadha. That was in the first century B.C. Four hundred years had passed since Buddha's Nirvana, but the Master's words were impressive, penetrating and repetitive, full of beautiful similes that were never forgotten. And faithfully the Guru had them handed down to the Chela, the teacher to the pupil. Heavy monsoon clouds approach. Storms shake the jungle giants and scatter scarlet hibiscus blossoms over the sleeper. Then a clap of thunder, just as on that far off full-moon in the Spring month of Vaishakha.

Sigiriya (Plates 14—16)

The fifth century, from which the Sigiriya frescos (and the Mahawansa) date, was also a zenith of artistic and intellectual development on the Indian mainland. At the court of the Guptas the poet Kalidasa wrote, "The servant of the goddess Kali" (Durga) and the reliefs on the Dhamek-Stupa at Sarnath form a climax in man's creative art. The stucco plaster (Chunam), which was then painted, is one-half inch thick and consists of a double layer— the top one hard and smooth as marble. After the surrender of the fortress, the royal household returned to Anuradhapura (which ceded its importance to Polonnaruwa only in the eighth century) and the palace on the "lion rock" fell into decay. The Sigiriya frescos and the somewhat older ones at Ajanta (see page 27)—the product, one may guess, of a tradition of untold generations of artists—are the only surviving monuments of old Indian painting and are as such extremely important.

Polonnaruwa (Plates 9—11)

This was Ceylon's capital from the mid-eighth century until the thirteenth century. In 1907-8, several full bronze statues, about forty inches high dating from about the twelfth or thirteenth century and probably imported from southern India, were discovered near the Hindu temple (Siva Devalé)—figures similar to the dancing Siva on the last plate of this book. The round temple (Wata Dagé) with its central Dagoba and its raised, encircling processional pathway vividly calls to mind the semi-globular earthern mounds of the Sanchi-Stupas. The outer ramparts are about shoulder high. In front of the four entrances lie moonstones, similar to those reproduced in Plate 17. Guard-stones protect the ascent. The balustrade is formed by a volute that grows like a tongue out of the jaws of a mythical beast. Plate 10 reproduces only the right half of the "Black Rock" (Gal-Kalugal). The forty-five-feet long reposing statue shows the sacred emblem, a spoked wheel, on the soles of both feet. The disciple standing next to the Master (Ananda) is twenty-three feet tall. These immense statues were rediscovered in 1820 and can be compared only to the giant bas-reliefs at Mamallapuram (Plate 40).

Anuradhapura (Plates 12, 13, 17)

The town's golden age took place about the time of the birth of Christ, but it had been the capital since 437 B.C. When the kings removed to Polonnaruwa, dense jungle enclosed it and tiger and bear took possession of the place. Monasticism was powerful in the ancient Anuradhapura, and perhaps the "Brazen Palace" that Dutugemunu erected in 161 B.C. was no royal residence but the chief monastery of the town. Despite the close ties between monasticism and the crown here and in Burma, the Buddhist monks never interfered in state affairs, and despite their considerable influence on the people, they have never striven after worldly power.

Mihintale (Plate 8)

Numerous pilgrims annually tread the via sacra among the many traces of ancient temples and hermitages. Beneath the overhanging face of the rock, which offers a never-to-be-forgotten view of the extensive jungle, one seeks the hermitage where Mahinda, the royal monk and son of the great Asoka, lived in self-chosen poverty.

We descend the steps shown in Plate 17 and take leave of Ceylon, which has justly been designated the precious pearl in Mother India's ear. Vijaya, offspring of a union between an Aryan princess and a lion, is the mythical founder of the "Lion Island," where hidden in the bush the last remnants of an aboriginal people still live. Pagodas and palm trees tower. The proud, silvery talipot and the useful coconut palm, which seeks the coastland, longingly strain for the surf, to savor the invigorating, salt-tanged air. There are fig trees, each one forming a small grove of its own, and the green "geysers" of the bamboos. Tortoises are found in the temple pools, the village streams and in the courtyard of the rest-house. One can pick them up quite unconcernedly. Animals are tame and trusting when man follows Ahimsa's commandment: "Thou shalt not kill nor harm any living creature."

INDIA

Madurai (Plates 19, 20, 25)

From afar one is greeted by the nine giant towers of the southern Banaras. They breathe the monumental calm of Egyptian pylons. As we come closer so that the eye can distinguish details, the slightly concave pyramidal surfaces are transformed into a raging tumult (Plate 25). All Western standards fail us here. The tropical, fruitful, myth-making power of the Hindu spirit, which created a pantheon that to us seems quite inexplicable, has its expression in stone. As the myths flourish, defying all dogma, impossible to compress into one system, so the builders of these divine towers disregarded every building regulation, every rational principle. The figures issuing from the minds of the craftsmen throng out of the inside of the pyramids, prolific as the seed of tropical fruit, to seek a place in the sun. However strange the towers may seem to us, they are symbolic of their environment; they are the final expression of the spirit that created them.

These towers were not yet standing when a Jesuit father set foot on the soil of Mandurai in 1606. Rome had sent to the stronghold of Brahminism a most eminent apologist, a man of the old Roman aristocracy, of most noble disposition, Robert de Nobili. His goal was fundamentally the same as that of the men whose sole ornaments are the linen shoulder strap and the seal on the brow which daily renew their duty to their god: to live in the spirit and in truth, to penetrate to the real truth behind external appearance, to penetrate beyond the transitory to the eternal. Robert de Nobili was the first man with both religious training and knowledge of their language to appear among these people. He was able to discuss with them the ultimate question: the absorption of the immaterial individual into the supreme soul, the Brahma. Both Catholicism and Brahminism had been purged—the one through Lutheran, the other through Buddhist criticism. Both fundamentally share the doctrine of the Karma. A witty Englishman once asked: "Did Nobili convert the Brahmins or did *they* convert *him?*" We do not know the answer, but his influence must have been considerable on the court as well as the clergy. Tradition has it that Tirumala Nayak, the builder of the mighty temple (Plate 20) was entombed alive by the priests, who were not allowed to spill blood, because he was in danger of falling under the influence of the Jesuits. With reference to the countries of Asia with their culture dating back many thousands of years some authorities are of the opinion that the inhabitants of these lands stood intellectually, morally and spiritually far above those who came to teach them. That may have been the case with many missionaries, but in Madurai equals encountered each other. A tragic fate prevented Robert de Nobili from appearing before Akbar, who on his mother's side was a direct descendant of the great Genghis Khan and a man of Solomonic wisdom, who summoned Jews, Christians and Brahmins to his court for discussions so that he could examine all beliefs and retain the best. The philosopher-king died while the great Jesuit was on his way to India. Robert de Nobili, the "Apostle to the Brahmins," who in dress and mode of life had become completely Indian, died as octogenarian in 1656 in Mylapore, a suburb of Madurai.

The Gopuram reproduced on Plate 25 is 150 feet high. Its upper end is terminated by a cylindrical-shaped roof, framed by festoons of flames at the gabled sides. Strangely enough, the pyramids do not tower over the sacred shrines but over the gates. The practically legendary proportions of the fanaticism of the Madurai priests is demonstrated by these temple photographs, which are only a small selection from more than a hundred. That the Brahmin succeeded in maintaining and consolidating his power without any widespread, organized hierarchy, without use of temporal forces, merely confirms the fact that India has a far greater respect for the spiritual than any other nation in the world.

Rameswaram (Plate 18)

The temple, whose richly sculptured corridors joined end to end would measure a total distance of three-quarters of a mile, is situated on a palm-shaded island named by the god-like hero Rama. Rama's separation from his faithful wife, Sita, whom the wicked giant-king Ravana had carried off to Lanka, his grief and their final reunion make up the theme of the Indian Odyssey, attributed to a bard named Valmiki and dating from the sixth or fifth century B.C. Just as the separation and final reunion of Krishna and the beautiful Radha has been symbolically interpreted as the separation of the human soul from the Divine and its final reunion, so this myth also contains deep religious, mystical references; thus we often encounter Ramayana scenes depicted on temple walls (cf. Somnathpur).

Kalugumalai (Plate 24)

The unfinished temple gives us a good idea of how the craftsmen of the Kailsa temple at Ellora worked on a large scale (see Plates 78, 79).

The Karur District (Plates 23, 27)

In Hinduism, as in all religions, the original ancient popular beliefs and superstitions remained alongside the "official" priest-protected dogmas. Hinduism was wise enough to tolerate these conceptions and tacitly incorporated them in its expandable Pantheon. Thus the Wild Horseman, who nightly rides round the peasants' fields and scares away the evil spirits, perhaps an aboriginal local diety, becomes the son of Siva.

Thiruwanaikawal near Trichinopoly
(Plate 26)

There are no references to the village deities depicted here to be found in the writings wherein the myths of the great gods have been given literary expression. Here, too, ago-old popular imagination created, primitive ideas found natural expression. "As each creature is, so likewise is his faith" (Bhagavadgita 17. Canto).

Sri Rangam (Plate 28)

At great festivals the heavy, wooden-horse-drawn processional chariot is pulled in triumph by a fanatical host of pilgrims, pouring in from every Indian province. At Kanarak in Orissa on the shore beside the surging sea rises the stone temple of the Sun-god, visible from afar. It reproduces, faithful even to the smallest detail, the shape of such a temple chariot. Hubs, cinctures, spokes of the huge wheels are chiseled as lovingly and delicately as if Master Jamnitzer had formed them in pure gold. This illusion becomes reality when the rays of the evening sun play on the creepers and figures. The gigantic chariot of the Sun-god is drawn by far-stepping, broad-chested horses. Verrocchio could not have lent them a nobler form.

Kumbakonam (Plate 29)

Every twelve years, so it is believed, the Ganges discharges some of its water subterraneously into the large temple pool of Kumbakonam, which is then overcrowded with bathing pilgrims and consequently rises a couple of inches. The last time this event was celebrated was in February, 1956. The temple tower reproduced here rises to the prodigious height of 146 feet—thereby only three feet less than the highest Gopuram in Madurai. The temple enclosures seldom lack a cow, which was pronounced sacred so that the ignorant peasant should not slaughter his most indispensable domestic animal. "The cow is sacred," says Ghandi, "for she is the mother of millions of Indians."

Chidambaram (Plate 30)

Ancient capital of the Chola dynasty that ruled in southern India from 907 until 1310, when Malik Kafur put an end to it (see page 19). The temple enclosure, surrounded by a high outside wall 1788 feet long and 1463 feet broad, owes its opulent form to King Hiranya Varna Chakravarti, whom a bath in the temple freed from leprosy. Two of the four Gopurams, 163 feet high, surpass the pylons of Madurai. The Hall of a Thousand Pillars in the Siva temple at Chidambaram can be compared favorably in size and beauty with the much-praised Hall of a Thousand Columns, Sahasrasthambha Mandapam, in Madurai.

Mamallapuram (Plates 31, 32, 40, 41)

When the Chinese scholar Hiuen Tsang was journeying through India in the second quarter of the seventh century (in the reign of the great King Harsha) the strip of coastland south of Madras belonged to King Narasimhavarman I, whose skill in wrestling had brought him the surname "Mahamalla." He founded the place that still bears his name: Mamallapuram (in Sanskrit, Mahabalipuram).

In a deep fissure over a thirty-four-foot high precipitous rock foamed a mountain torrent, now walled up and diverted (Plate 40). The artist turned this natural scenery into the greatest, most significant rock relief in the world. It was especially painful for the author to limit himself to a single picture because of lack of space. Coming from above (not visible in the picture) Nag and Nagaina, the Snake King and his Queen, writhe their way down into the pool below. From left and right all hasten to receive the blessing—men, gods, winged genii, the wise elephant and its young, the whole of Creation rejoices in the descent of the holy, blessing, dispensing Ganga, who in the distant Himalayas gushes forth out of Siva's locks. An ascetic venerates the god, who appears to be the emaciated old man in the doorway of the shrine. At his feet lie two deer. They feel themselves safe and secure, for one of them comfortably scratches himself. That the old master was not lacking in humor is demonstrated by a tomcat on the other side of the crevice, opposite the ascetic. Standing erect, he parodies the penetential exercises, while mice and rats dance round him. A

16

family of monkeys in raised sculpture (on extreme right and not visible in the picture) has lost interest in the proceedings and engages itself in activity that always gives great pleasure to children in the zoo.

Wherever a granite drift block laid, be it large or small, it was transformed into a work of art—an animal, a temple shrine. Seldom is the interior of the building completed, but wherever the craftsman could complete his work, he created something incomparable. The wall-covering "Minotauros" relief (Plate 41) far surpasses contemporary Western sculpture and the lion columns as interior and facade-supporting motifs precede ideas of Nicolo Pisano by six centuries. In the images for worship the Indian artist was bound by a hallowed tradition; in the bas-relief he could add personal touches. Therein lies the significance of the Mamallapuram bas-reliefs.

The Indian artist still believed in the spirits in the wind, the Dryas in the trees, the mountain demons and the nymphs of the spring. Because rock and stream were animated by divine forces it was easy for him to give these forces form and shape. Only Rodin felt again the pulsating life in stone that cries out for liberation through the artist's chisel. He who comes from a godless, soulless world would have noticed nothing further than a face of a cliff and a channel of water. To the Indian artist the waters of the torrent revealed the beneficial rule of the great goddess. And to the glory of the gods he transformed the surrounding drift blocks into places of veneration.

We stroll down to the shore (see the distant light-house in Plate 32). Slender palms and shady pines accompany us. The landscape is full of dedication and solitude, as is that of Olympia. On the shore towers an eighth-century temple, the only one that was built of individual stones in Western fashion. Lost in thought, it surveys the breakers (Plate 31). Perhaps the stone masons of Mamallapuram answered the call from across the sea, to Cambodia, or the far eastern islands south of the Equator, so that they could not complete their work here. Waves and sand-dunes have eradicated their names and their traces, but their work is imperishable—as imperishable as the Borobudur on Java and the enigmatic rock reliefs executed by Indian craftsmen on Bali.

Vellore (Plate 33)

Even he who finds it odd to use a rearing horse as a cornice support, i.e. constructively, will have to concede that the horses of Vellore can compete in boldness of movement and inner fire with the most famous monuments of this kind. Since Buddha's own horse, Kanthaka, on which "though still in full bloom, splendidly darkhaired, in the delight of happy youth, contrary to the wishes of his weeping and lamenting parents, he rode from home into homelessness, with shaven head and chin, dressed in faded garments." Since Buddha's own horse had gained a place in the plastic arts, the horse, unknown to the first settlers of Mohenjo Daro, has often been glorified, so the horses which like Caryatides are used as supports, do not hit out into space with their forefeet. To give them some support, the sculptor of Vellore created all kinds of fabled beasts under their hooves.

Chamundi Hill (Plate 34)

Two-thirds of the way up this 3,250-foot-high hill which forms a harmonious background for the spruce town of Mysore, is the Nandi bullock, carved out of the living rock in 1659. It stands sixteen feet high and has a magical effect, especially at night when it is softly illuminated and the contours of the hill are lit up by tousands of electric glow lamps. Also at Gyan Bapi at the Well of Knowledge in the sacred Banaras, a similar stone bull, symbol of fertility, keeps silent watch (Plate 49).

Tiruvannamalai (Plate 35)

This temple cannot compare in religious importance and artistic quality with those shown up to now, but the neighboring hill enables us to study its plan— that of a large Hindu temple. One walled courtyard is set within the next. Long and mysterious is the way which the Hindu must tread to reach the Holy of Holies. He must pass through ever fresh court-yards, more gates. In northern India (see also Plate 46) the tower always rises above the small, mysteriously dark Cella. In the South the *gates* are emphasized by tall, pyramidal towers. Living quarters for priests and pilgrims, pools and towers that are reflected in the water, together with the many shrines and chapels, make up a whole, confused town.

Seringapatam (Plate 36)

If the snake stones recall pre-Aryan animal worship, the gate visible in the background on the right is a reminder of modern events. On May 4, 1799, the courageous Tipu Sultan of Mysore, the son of Haidar Ali, was killed here at the second siege of Seringapatam. A soldier sought to tear away the wounded Sultan's bejewelled sword belt; the Sultan wounded his aggressor and the latter shot him down.

Somnathpur (Plates 37, 39)

The temple recalls a wrought gold jewel box. According to a Canaresian inscription at the entrance it was completed in 1270 by Soma, member of the royal family and mandatory minister of the Hoysala state. It has a star-shaped outline and each pyramid is serrated several times so that from morning to night beneath the rays of the moving sun the temple sparkles like a many-faceted precious stone. The craftsman who so cleverly included light and shadow in the whole concept also understood how to animate each surface through the interplay of light and darkness. Indeed he forced the very sun itself to provide the relief. All the figures are carved deeply into the stone; out of the resulting velvet-like darkness the ivory-colored marble gains a plastic contour that it is impossible even to indicate in a photograph (Plate 39). Amusing elephants in busy trot; richly ornamented men on horseback; involute, undulating creeper; scenes from the Ramayana epic; above, between pyramid-crowned columns, divine images and heraldic lions. The uppermost frieze is decorated with gods, musicians and lovers, and juts outward because of the occasional rounded benches inside.

In the ground plan of the temple drawn up by Jakanacharya, architecture and sculpture, which in modern buildings are often not harmoniously united, here practically become one. Forty statues are by Mallitamma. The artists of Mamallapuram modestly retire behind their work. As those of Somnathpur have left their signature, quite contrary to Indian artistic custom, it seems as if their contemporaries regarded their work as something really extraordinary. And yet the temple of Somnathpur is only one of many!

This modern age is loud in its praises of its bald concrete buildings. Is not a good deal of impotence—material and spiritual—hidden behind our modern "reality" so that we can no longer produce achievements such as the Gothic masters created out of the northern spirit and the masters of Somnathpur and Halebid created out of the Indian spirit? The star-shaped design and the attractive play of perpendicular bands of light and shadow produced by it were also used by the builder of the world's most beautiful minaret, the Kutb Minar in Delhi, which owes its existence to the caprice of a young girl who wished to see a far distant river from this spot.

Sravana Belgola (Plates 42, 43)

Each Indian landscape has its own perculiar character, its own sharply cut features. As the large clay horses are characteristic of the Karur district, so the huge, monolithic Jain statues on the mountain tops are perculiar to Kanara. Mahavira, the founder of the Jain religion, was a contemporary of Buddha's and spoke the same language, Magadhi. Mahavira is also concerned with the struggle with the ego, the struggle against passion, whose fruits are suffering as it is said in the thirteenth canto of the Bhagavadgita. Jina means "conqueror" and Mahavira "great Hero." Unwittingly we recall Buddha's simile: "If a man vanquish a thousand times a thousand men in battle and another overcomes only himself, so is the latter the greater conqueror."

The monolithic statue on Plate 42 was, according to the inscription, erected in 983 by Chamunda Raya and is the largest of its kind in the world. With a height of seventy-two feet, it exceeds Lederer's Bismarck statue in Hamburg by twenty-three feet. The statue is firmly rooted in the ground, but the thoughts of the holy man soar up into the clouds above. Hair style and solemn, serious expression are reminiscent of early Buddhist sculpture, as is the lotus blossom under the feet that are considerably shortened below the knee and from a distance obscured from view by porticos (pillared halls). Head and body were intended to be as large as possible to be visible from the greatest distances in the surrounding countryside. The total height was predetermined because the statue is hewn out of a needle of rock which a caprice of Nature had placed on the summit of a mountain. Every twenty-five years the statue is annointed with ghi and therefore looks quite new, as if the stone masons had put on the finishing touches but yesterday. The similarity of Jainism and Buddhism is attested by old inscriptions which relate the famous Maurya king Chandragupta to Bhadra Bahu, a Skruta kevala, and his grandson Asoka, to Sravana Belgola, where Bhadra Bahu died in the fourth century B.C.

Halebid (Plates 38, 44, 45)

The Hoysaleswara temple in the neighboring Halebid (Hale means "old" and bidu "residence" in Canaresian) is described by Fergusson as "one of the most marvelous exhibitions of human labor to be found even in the patient East." The circulating base friezes (Plate 38), whose number is here increased by bandelets of birds and sea elephants out of whose mouths tendrils grow, have an average length of 700 feet. The bands joined together would thus cover several miles, and everything—the trappings of the horses, the ornaments of the two thousand small elephants, the upper canopies of trees—all is wrought with the attention to detail of an Augsburg goldsmith or a Tyrolean wood carver. Here too the lowest bandelet is reserved for the elephant, the wisest inhabitant of the jungle, the Indian's most trusted friend. Since ancient times he has been Indra's mount (Plate 81); respectfully he does reverence to the sacred fig tree at the Stupa gate of Sanchi. The roof of Hoysaleswara, a twin temple dedicated to Siva and his wife, Parvati, was never completed. In 1310 the town fell into the hands of Mohammedans under Malik Kafur.

In front of the temple, Ganesa, the son of Siva and Parvati, shakes his head significantly. The craftsman who knew how to chisel the frieze elephants so delicately that they resembled ivory carvings was also a supreme master of monumental sculpture. Even one who is accustomed to seeing wisdom personified in the likeness of the virgin goddess Pallas Athene must agree that the proverbial wisdom of the Indian elephant has found convincing expression in the noble arch of the mighty brow (see the Ganes temple in Vijayanagar, Plate 50, which with its elegant, Ionian-like columns is among the most lovely buildings of southern India).

Belur (Plate 48)

A book of this size would not suffice to do justice to this temple which the Hoysala king Vishnu Vardhana erected after he had exchanged the Jain faith for the Vishnu religion in 1139. Jakanacharya, whom we already encountered active in Halebid and Somnathpur, surpassed himself at Belur. 28 large windows, closed by sculptured marble slabs, and each one different. The light falls through open stars, through creeper patterns; other windows depict mythological scenes and an abundance of figures. The noblest example of Gothic Cathedral architecture seems shabby by comparison with Jakanacharya's superb work. "The amount of labor which each displays is such as never was bestowed on any surface of equal extent in any building in the world" says Fergusson, the "Winckelmann" of India's history of Art.

Gracefully moving maidens support the beams, whose weight is lessened by their decorative charm. They are at their loveliest early in the morning or in the evening, when the slanting rays of the sun play on the dark stone so that it gleams like pure bronze: musicians, dancers in attractive variations, a splendid, vivacious archeress. Should anyone believe that he can study anatomy from the statues either here or at Palampet, he has completely misunderstood the artist's intentions. Jakanacharya did not want to demonstrate anatomy but to reveal the flexibility and movement of the feminine body in his temple dancers. Just as the Indian philosopher has his roots in the metaphysical, in the world beyond external appearance, so the artist was never as captivated by the forms of natural phenomena as to have merely copied them (there is not a single Indian portrait painter). The Indian artist always abstracted the spiritual element from the things of the physical world and sought to interpret it in its profoundest cosmic relations.

Lakkandi (Plates 49, 51)

Here too where temple, pools and fountains (Baoli) are shaded by immense trees of the jungle, Jakanacharya is alleged to have worked. Frequently a black chlorite stone served as building material which, highly polished, has a deceptive similarity to bronze, clearly shown by the tortile column in Plate 51.

Badami (Plate 54)

Unfortunately, lack of space prevents us from reproducing the heroic landscape on whose heights stand the temples of the ancient Chalukya capital, in whose flanks their chapels are cut. The reproduced cave dates from the 6th century and is dedicated to the Brahmin religion built two centuries earlier as is the one at Elephanta (Plate 72). It is lighter than

19

the latter and the majority of Buddhist rock temples and monasteries. Six thirteen-feet high quadrilateral pillars ornamented with medallions and two pilasters support the portico. Shaft and ceiling are connected by saddle beam-like sculptures. The couple directly facing the spectator can easily be interpreted as Siva and Parvati. The huge, wall-covering sculpture in the background shows Narayan, enthroned on a snake whose crest is spread out like an aureole behind him. The corresponding symmetrical figure behind the spectator shows Vishnu in his incarnation as a lion (see the Narsingh image on Plate 60).

Pattadakal (Plate 46)

It is only nine and one-half miles from Badami to Pattadakal, but the bullock-cart with its creaking disc-wheels takes more than four hours because of the deep ruts in the road despite the efforts of the driver, who squats patiently on the shaft. The 7th or 8th century temples are with a single exception built in Dravidian style, which stresses the horizontal. This building, however (Plate 46), could just as easily stand in Bhubaneswar or Khajuraho. The tower (Sikhara) of the North Indian temple curves convexly and always rises over the Cella, whereas the South Indian Gopuram, when not straight-edged, curves concavely and, as we have already seen, crowns the *gates*. The neck of the Sikhara is narrowed and forms a pleasing transition from the square cross-section to the rounded form, into which the ascending, parabolically curved lines flow organically. A flat coussinet, Amalaka, which is ribbed like the capitals in the cave of Elephanta, forms the harmonious conclusion. One who contemplates the silhouette of the reproduced temple of Pattadakal attentively feels transported to the distant past, when sacred shrines were made of bent elastic bamboo canes stuck into the ground in square design and held together at the top by coconut fibre—in just the same fashion as the human huts.

Aiholi (Plate 56)

The Durga temple, probably dating from the sixth century, abounds in beautiful sculpture. The lion would do honor to Saint Mark's Square in Venice.

Vijayanagar (Plates 47, 50, 52, 53, 55, 58-61)

The year before Malik Kafur captured Halebid, he invested the Hindu fortress of Warangal (see Plate 57, 66), which did not fall, however, until fourteen years later when the warlike Muhammad-ibn-Tughlaq appeared before the gates. Two brothers, Bukka and Harihara, left Warangal and founded a new town on the Thungabhadra, which they named Vijayanagar, "Town of Victory." It prospered for two and a quarter centuries until the frightful battle of Talicota brought its splendors to an end. The violent battle was fought on January 23, 1565, when allied Deccan sultans engaged the Hindus on the battle-worn plains between the Thungabhadra and Kistna rivers. Not until the First World War was this battle equalled in the number of troops and victims. From the immense size of the Mohammedan troops we may gauge the power of the Vijayanagar kings. The Venetian traveler Cesar Frederick (see p. 9) saw "Bezenagar" two years after its fall and estimated its perimeter to be twenty-four miles, greater than the walled perimeter of Peking. The Portuguese traveler Domingo Paes, who visited the town at the beginning of the sixteenth century, tells of streets as broad as the lists, and the ruins endorse their statements. According to Abdur Razzak, who was Persian ambassador to the court of the Vijayanagar kings around the middle of the fifteenth century, their kingdom already extended at that time from the Kistna river to Cape Comorin. Krishnaraja (1509 to 1530) entertained friendly relations with Goa. We learn that he asked the governor to send him Portuguese stone masons, and the Portuguese viceroy hastened to comply with his wishes and sent him Joao della Ponte, "a great master in stone." Paes also left us personal characteristics of the great Vijayanagar Emperor. Of athletic stature, he would ride around the town every morning.

For five months, some sources say even ten, the Mohammedans endeavored to destroy the town. They did not succeed—anymore than the warriors of Kubla Khan succeeded in obliterating the recollection of Pagan. Of the throne room, which we must imagine as a gilded wooden hall similar to those in the palaces of Mandalay and Anuradhapura, only the granite bases remain, but even they are still of enormous dimensions. The bas-reliefs (Plate 55) vividly recall Assyria: warriors, horses, elephants, camels, dancers, musicians; tigers, antelope and wild-boar hunts—standing, on foot, mounted, in short, everything that can gladden a king's heart.

A special wing of the palace surrounded by a high wall with tall corner towers whose windows were once closed by delicate wooden grills was reserved for the Emperor's wives (Plate 53). From there where there was always a cooling breeze the curious harem beauties could observe the life und bustle of the court without being seen themselves.

The Arab traveler Ibn Batuta, who visited India in the 14th century and was a keen observer, recounts the following: "The burning of widows counts as a praiseworthy act amongst the Indians, but it is not obligatory. If, however, a widow allows herself to be cremated, her whole kin achieves renown thereby and her fidelity is highly praised. Yet she is not obliged to let herself be cremated if it is against her wishes." The widow's cremation stones (Maha-sati-kal), reproduced on Plate 58, depict women with right arm raised in an extremely odd, formal fashion. It is bent at the elbow, fingers outstretched. Perhaps the dead blesses the venerators of the stela, or perhaps it signifies that she has sacrificed all "arm and hand" to her dead husband. Sun and moon are called upon as witnesses and are added in relief.

Annually in autumn a nine-day feast was celebrated when the subject rulers brought their tribute. Then the huge eleven-domed Imperial elephant stables were not sufficiently large for the demand. How tiny in comparison to the magnificently preserved stables are the royal mews of Europe. In order to water the mounts of foreign visitors a cyclopic forty-two foot trough was placed in the palace yard. It is hewn out of a single rock and as perfect as if it had come from the stone mason but yesterday!

Sir Thomas Roe, in India shortly after Queen Elizabeth had granted a charter to the Honorable East India Company on December 31, 1600, describes the ceremony of Tula-purusha-dana: At special occasions such as coronations and eclipses of sun or moon, the king would let himself be weighed in full armor—instead of weights, gold was thrown into the scales and was later distributed. Perhaps this custom is the last echo of a self-sacrifice that the king offered to the gods in gray antiquity. Krishnaraja's successor even let himself be weighed in pearls. The triumphal-arch-like gateway on whose lintel the scales were hung still stands today. The laudable custom is not yet extinct, as the author could personally testify

on January 19, 1936, when H. H. the Aga Khan celebrated the golden jubilee of his nomination as Imam. His weight was balanced by 9500 gold tolas —equal to 3 Lakh and 35,000 rupees—a sum of more than $ 125,000 (it is a point of honor on such occasions to be weighed in full dress, i.e. in full armor and then to round off the weight).

A few steps away from the uncouth lion-man with the protruding eyes and the hideous jaws, which represents Vishnu (Plate 60), Siva, the great god of procreation and his wife Durga, are worshipped under their symbols, the Lingam (phallus) and the Yoni (vulva). These symbols, which represent the natural instincts of humanity, are in their giant proportions a worthy counterpart to the lion-man, Narsingh Avatar.

That the masons of Vijayanagar were also capable of delicate chiseling is demonstrated by the stone temple chariot in the courtyard of the Vithoba temple (Plate 61) that was completed in 1521, seven years before the lion-headed Vishnu, in the reign of Krishnaraja. The joints are so invisibly fine, the nine heavy blocks so carefully polished, that former travelers described the monument as monolithic. I have encountered similarly skillful treatment of stone only in the Propylaea in Athens, but it was easier for the Attic craftsman. He worked in finely-grained Pentelikon marble, not in coarse Deccan granite.

Amidst a sea of ruins towers a lonely Nagaina (see Plate 52), hands folded beneath the uplifted bosom, the snake in its good-willed expression. Once the great god was allowed to rest from the sun in the shadow of her widespread crest. Sadly the goddess surveys the place formerly so full of life. Rama Rajah sent 750,000 foot soldiers, 100,000 cavalry against the allied Mohammedans. But the latter had more than six hundred cannon, cleverly hidden by 2,000 archers. Their roar created a panic amongst the Hindu elephants, which spread to the whole army. 100,000 men were killed; the ninety-year-old Emperor had his head struck off and placed on a spear as a victors' trophy. That was the end of the Imperial glory of Vijayanagar. Monkeys carrying their young under their bellies chase screeching along deserted corridors, swing through empty window casements, and pull faces at the traveler, frightening him by their number and their impertinent curiosity.

"It is noticeable that always the same things are described and photographed: those to be found on the normal tourists' routes and that arouse their attention most. As for innumerable temples situated away from the main lines of communication and which contain most interesting objects, they have remained practically unknown" (Jouveau-Dubreuil in *Archéologie du Sud de l'Inde*). As no work exists in the German language that mentions the old Imperial town on the Thungabhadra (which ceremoniously celebrated the 6th centenary of its foundation on Christmas, 1936) and as also no illustrated English book does justice to the importance of her monuments, Vijayanagar and its checkered fate have been dealt with more fully in illustration and in text than would normally be expected in a volume such as this. Just as the Hoysala temples in the present state of Mysore—Somnathpur, Halebid, Belur—speak their own language, inimitable in its lyric beauty, just as the buildings of Bijapur and Golconda bear their own peculiar stamp, so Vijayanagar has also formed its own style, determined by the psyche of its artists and the peculiarity of the material with which they worked. It is interesting to compare the Jakanacharya temples with those of Vijayanagar. For this the traveler needs weeks; the reader, merely a few minutes. On the one hand, an art that is, for some, already too refined—as the Shah Jahan's palaces in Delhi; on the other, a half-barbaric art, in some instances almost gross.

Vijayanagar's harbor was Goa. The "Goa dourado" that Camoens celebrates flourished as long as the Vijayanagar empire prospered. Once Goa's influence extended "ad extremas Orientis oras"—beyond the Malabar ports to Malacca and Macao. When the Mohammedans seized possession of Vijayanagar, the fever seized hold of "Golden Goa." Sad, lamenting and accusing sound the bells when they are rung occasionally for the great festivals. How often did their pitiless metal proclaim the burnings of heretics in the days of the Inquisition! At the Ribeira dos Viceroys towers a palm-shaded gateway. On the riverside it bears the coat-of-arms of Vasco da Gama, who landed on the Malabar coast on May 20, 1498. Above the back entrance, witness of the torture of suspected witches and heretics, is a "saint" who tramples on a "heathen." Portuguese colonialism, naked und undisguised. Today Goa is a **dead city** —deserted and ghostly lie the streets.

Tadpatri (Plate 62)

The most beautiful expression of Vijayanagar Art was wrought in Tadpatri, founded in 1485. The Rameswara temple remained unfinished, like many of our most splendid cathedrals. Whereas the plastic ornament on the Gopurams of southern India is limited to the pyramidal slopes (see Plate 25) the perpendicular bases at Tadpatri also bear rich plastic ornament. Unfortunately, the priests have buried all the subtleties under a thick coating of plaster which, to make things worse, is decorated in loud, vertical red and white stripes. But even this disfiguring, zebra-like coating has not succeeded in obliterating the beauty of the relief. Relaxed, with legs crossed, stands the graceful Yakshi on the back of a Makara, out of whose wide-open jaws flowering creeper twines itself. How the maiden's well-shaped arms entwine the curl of the creeper, becoming part of it. This indicates a really great artist. Other presentations in the unfinished archway are more opulent and show birds singing in the curl of the tendril above the girl's head. All life is one; man and plant spring from the same origins. Because he was completely convinced of this truth, the unknown craftsman of Tadpatri knew how to blend them so convincingly, the gloriously blooming maiden and the exuberant, growing creeper.

Palampet (Plate 63)

We are in the former kingdom of the Nizam, which we leave after Gulbarga and enter again at Aurangabad in order to see Ellora and Ajanta. The nearest railway station is forty miles away and the lonely trek through the jungle not without danger; yet even one single column would amply reward the trouble! Perhaps the temple is so well preserved because it lies off the highway and tourist routes. Coquettish little maidens, petrified Devadases, dance around the entrance to the shrine and support its roof from outside. They are perhaps even more graceful than the Caryatides of Belur—a little too desirous to please, to show the spectator a pose that they have practised in front of the mirror to be particularly suited to displaying their charms. In Palampet, too, black basalt was used, which, highly polished, burnishes like bronze (see Plate 51).

Warangal (Plate 57, 66)

These lions with threatening, upraised paws were not able to drive off the Mohammedans. Yet they give a good idea of the magnificence and size of the old Hindu monuments. Judging by the four triumphal-archlike gates that today mourn in solitude amidst tilled fields, the square market place of Warangal could have competed with the fora of Imperial Rome.

Hyderabad D. (Plates 64, 65)

The city, situated on the Musi and about equal distance from Bombay and Madras, with a population of more than a million, is the fourth largest in India. It was founded in 1589 by the fifth Kutb Shahi of Golconda. Immeasurable was the legendary wealth of the Kutb Shahi kings. The "stones of Golconda" are still proverbial today. From the mines of Kollur in the Krishna district comes the Koh-i-noor, "mountain of light," which today adorns the English royal crown, and formerly sparkled on Akbar's tomb in Sikandra (see p. 11).

The diamond cutters of Golconda enjoyed world renown, as do those of Amsterdam today; the choicest jewels from every land found their way here: turquoise from Tibet, green jade from China; Persia sent onyx, Ceylon sapphires, Socotra red coral and Rameswaram pearls. The mighty gateway with its four minaret-like towers, each 185 feet high (Plate 64), is one of the oldest monuments of the city of Hyderabad and was erected in 1591.

Gulbarga (Plate 71)

Founded when Muhammad Tughlaq Shah was Emperor of Delhi (1325—1351), the Bahmani state later broke up into 5 kingdoms, of which Bijapur, Golconda and Ahmadnagar were the most important. One can adduce the size and beauty of the other buildings from this archway. Banda Nawaz, member of the Chishti family (see Plate 97), came to Gulbarga in 1413 in the reign of Firoz Shah, the builder of the Great Mosque. Unlike all other large Indian mosques that always consist of an open courtyard with a narrow, covered Liwan built into the western side, the Jami Masjid is completely covered over, and the legend that it was built by a Moorish builder from Cordoba is not so unlikely.

Bijapur (Plate 67—69)

On the ramparts of Bijapur stands a giant cannon of bell-metal bronze. It is fourteen feet long, has a circumference of thirteen and one-half feet, and a caliber of twenty-eight inches. Muhammad Bin Husain Rumi, a Turk, proudly indentified himself as the craftsman who in the year 956 of the Hegira (1551 in Admadnagar) cast this howitzer which far surpasses the largest Krupp, Scoda and Armstrong mortars of the Second World War. The highly-polished mouth depicts the jaws of a monster swallowing an elephant. Malik-i-Maidan, the "Lord of the Battlefield," is alleged to have taken part in the battle of Talicota and through his dreadful roar caused the enemy elephants to charge their own (Hindu) ranks. Bijapur was the chief heritage of the Vijayanagar Empire and flourished until 1686, when it fell into the hands of the frightful Aurangzib, who brought all Indian glory to an end and made the land ripe for foreign domination. Bijapur (Vijaya-pura) in its name "City of Victory" continues the tradition of Vijayanagar. It owes its prosperity to the Turk Yusaf Khan son of Amurath II of Anatolia, whose mother brought him to India to save him from the customary fate of all young Oriental princes. He planted on the domes of Bijapur a generation later the crescent moon that had shone since 1453 over the church of St. Sapientia in Constantinople, where it still stands today.

Sultan 'Ali 'Adil Shah I led the Bijapur contingent at Talicota. The Great Mosque, which proclaimed Islam's victory, proves how vast was the booty. It enabled even his successors to realise each of his dreams in stone. The power of Bijapur was tremendous; it extended as far as Goa, and even at sea lay a strong sultanic fleet.

The Taj-Sultana, wife of his successor, Ibrahim II, employed a Persian craftsman to erect her tomb. Malik Sandal completed his work before the building of the Taj Mahal was begun. Never was noble womanhood so graciously expressed in a work of architecture. Calligraphic verses of the Koran become ornamentation and sink into sweet dreams (Plate 68); dead-gold marble arabesques and azure background blend harmoniously. The central cupola grows out of a wreath of leaves like a swelling lotus bud. This motif is repeated on the minarets. They have no spiral stairway for the prayer-caller, but like the central cupola, are purely ornamental to emphasize the splendid outward appearance. As the central cupola motif is echoed on the various turrets, so out of the root of the minaret grow more decorative turrets. Stone chains, hewn out of one piece with an ingenious, filigree pendant that encloses a movable stone ball, sway in the breeze. Much has been ruined: Aurangzib had made the edifice into his head-quarters when he beseiged Bijapur, and the Sultan's artillery was forced to put the mausoleum under fire.

Formerly the tomb was surrounded by a park as beautiful as the garden round the tomb of the prophet of Medina, the famous Rauza. "It had borrowed its beauty from the Garden of Paradise." Flowering bushes of jasmine, in which birds twittered, singing fountains—the whole more like an habitation for the living than a mausoleum for the dead! Ibrahim died before his wife, and the same tomb encloses them both, just as the Taj Mahal in Agra was to unite husband and wife in death: the Empress Arjmand Banu Begum, the "Chosen One of the Palace," and Shah Jahan, who did not succeed in building his own tomb because his son Aurangzib held him prisoner, fearing that his inheritance would be diminished by new and costly buildings.

When Ibrahim II's successor, Muhammad, began to plan his tomb (the later Bijapur sultans thought more of their own glorification than that of Allah) he realised that the Ibrahim Rauza was not to be surpassed in its lyric, feminine beauty. So he erected an edifice of such power and manly size, such weight and severity and unheard-of boldness, that this accomplishment was never again attained, let alone surpassed (Plate 67). The monument is simple as are all great things of this world—a walled square outline of 654 square feet, founded on living rock, and above it, a cupola 143 feet in diameter. No columns, no pillars are inside; none of the supports are outside that so disfigure the Sophia Mosque. How does the architect deal with the cupola? He cast it in concrete, the pressure of which pushes vertically downward. The mixture remains a secret that accompanied the unknown craftsman to his grave. The minarets are in the shape of compressed, octagonal eight-floored stairway-towers added to the corners of the square whereby the edifice gains in compactness. Invitingly the monumental gates open, in stature far beyond the earthly. High above them, on the outside, runs a gallery which projects 11$^1/_2$ feet. Inside around the foot of the cupola, accessible from the seventh floor of the tower, runs a second gallery, likewise without any supports and without use of iron, which projects so far that a car could comfortably drive round it! A whispered word

is echoed tenfold by the opposite wall of the cupola so loud that one is frightened by the sound of one's own voice. Amazed, we look up to the zenith of the dome, that is undecorated, like the rest of the edifice. It soars 115 feet above the floor; the walls are nine feet thick at the vertex, ten feet at the beginning of the dome. "The sky was amazed when it saw the arch of this edifiice—a second sky had been created!" We can well understand that the thirty-year-long reign of Muhammad (1626—1656) was not sufficient to complete the work!

Karli (Plates 73, 74)

At Hotgi Junction we reach the Madras-Bombay line of the Central Railway (formerly the Great Indian Peninsula Railway). Six hours express journey to Poona, where a heavy electric engine was put at the head of the train. The waters which in the rainy season poured devastatingly through the gates of the Westghat, have been dammed and converted to electric energy. Soon we reach Lonavla.

Whoever enters for the first time the early Buddhist rock temple of Karli, which is worked into the Westghat at the point of the coastal plain, imagines himself in an early Christian basilica (Plate 74). The same requirements produced the same kind of construction. In the wooden rafters, which below the self-supporting stone vaulting are of no constructive significance, remains the echo of old wooden buildings. The columns, with kneeling elephants over faceted bells on which youths and maidens sit in confiding embrace, recall Asoka's edict columns (see p. 29) and seem to be influenced by Persian example. If the shafts of the columns appear to stand in a kind of bulging bucket, this too is a distant echo of ancient wooden construction technique: in order to protect them from greedy white ants, the wooden column was placed in a large clay bucket which could always be filled with water when the need arose—in the same way as the modern tropical tourist fills his empty tins with water after he has placed the wooden table legs in them.

Where in Christian churches there is the altar, in which reliques were often kept, is a large, round reliquary, around which seven slender pillars stand in semi-circle, connecting the thirty columns of the central nave. Just as the early Christians contented themselves with symbols—Christ monograms, fish and lamb—so the early Buddhists used the wheel of the law, the tree of perception, the semiglobular reliquary, around which seven slender pillars stand for an image of the Buddha in the rock temple at Karli, which may go back to the pre-Christian era. Founder couples, far larger than life-size, are engraved in the entrance wall: solidly healthy and sensual women, with wide open, astonished, child-like eyes, widespread hips and breasts distended with milk. Woman in her motherly aspect! Feminine beauty is synonymous with fertility for the Indian (see Plate 16).

Brahminism, recalled to new life by Shankara eleven centuries ago, took root here in the old refuge of Buddhism too; in front of the Chaitya of Karli, Siva is worshipped in a small temple, without anyone looking askance at the Buddhist pilgrims. In Ellora too, they all lived peaceably together—Buddhist, Jain and Siva worshippers!

Kondane (Plate 75)

Where in Karli the wooden girth inserted into the rock vaulting made it seem likely that former wooden constructions were transmuted into a more durable material, this is clearly the case in Kondane. Here the front part of the vaulting is ribbed *lengthwise*. Only a carpenter works thus with lathing and protruding balconies, as can be seen in on the stone façade of Kondane. (In the neighbouring Bhaja, whose cave dates from the second century B. C., the stone pillars do not incline inwards at all, as do wooden supports.)

Elephanta (Plate 72)

The island, named by the Portuguese after a rock with the silhouette of an elephant, lies only six miles from Bombay pier, and yet there are "globe trotters" who know the Taj Mahal Hotel and the quartiers where Kama is to be found but do not bother about "the old grotto" where "nothing happens anyway." Whoever steps from the bright daylight into the cave, which dates from the eighth century (as does the Kailasa temple in Ellora), is at first so blinded that he sees nothing. Gradually a huge, three-fold head rises out of the depths of the cave. On the middle head towers a tall tiara, and costly ornaments glitter on the breast. Although the image is quite transcendental, belonging to a supernatural world in its meditative absorption, its lips are full and sensual, especially on the right head which has there-

fore been interpreted as Siva's wife, Parvati (her marriage to the god is presented on a gigantic relief on the right side). As the central head represents Siva as Creator and the one on the left as Destroyer, the enigmatic face on the right that bends over a lotus blossom is probably Siva the Preserver. The bust is nineteen feet high and is guarded left and right by giant Dwarpals. Seldom has an artist dared to touch on the profoundest enigmas of the cosmos. In the Trimurti of Elephanta—which is unearthly and yet so earthly that we expect to hear their breathing— lies the whole cosmos, as in the fire ring of the dancing Siva at the conclusion of this book.

Kanheri (Plate 76)

This cave too lies on an island not far from Bombay—if one applies the scale of a land that is as large as half of Europe. When the Buddhists no longer felt at ease on the mainland, many of them went over to Salsette, which is still covered by dense jungle today. A hundred and nine caves remind us of them. The oldest go back to the second century A. D., but the majority are of a later date. One cave (Number three according to the official enumeration) dates from the sixth century and is apparently an imitation of Karli. The same donor couples are here comprised in huge double-reliefs—the women fertile, intellectually uncomplicated, as we know them from Karli. On both narrow ends of the portico are Buddhist statues of unusual size. Doubtless they are later additions, and the artistic abilities of the stone masons were limited; yet the place is not without effect. The solemn jungle solitude, the sea gleaming in the distance fill the soul with a gentle calm. I have often stood up here, listening to the sea breezes and looking at the sparkling stars. And the heavily hanging, giant hand was raised meaningfully as that of the Preacher Anslo, whom Rembrandt has immortalised—entreating, teaching, blessing: "There is no fire as hot as passion, no demon as bad as hate; there is no trap like delusion, no current like desire. Desires are like the fangs of a snake ... He who controls rising anger like a cart that goes the wrong way, him I call a true driver; another only holds the reins ... Work without ceasing towards perfection!" And the words of the Indian sage blend with the testament of the greatest German, who promises salvation to him that always strives to attain it.

Sinnar (Plate 95)

The reproduced temple, built and named after Rao Govinda, dates from the beginning of the twelfth century and attracts also through the solemn beauty of its position.

Aurangabad (Plate 70)

We are again in the former state of Nizam, which before the new division of India was as large as Italy. In a mausoleum, which is a cheap thoughtless imitation of the Taj Mahal in Agra, in ignoble material with weak decadent art, lies Aurangzib's wife Rabi'a Daurani. The Mecca gate and bridge, whose age is now impossible to determine, still breathe a certain strength and greatness.

Before going on to Ellora, let us glance at the tomb of the Emperor Aurangzib. Following the strict laws of the Koran, his tomb of Puritan simplicity, is open, exposed to sun and rain. Only the Nizam later surrounded it with a marble railing. Here lies the contemporary of Louis XIV, his own father's jailer, after a reign that was both long and calamitous (1658—1707) despite warlike victories against Bijapur (1686) and Golconda (1687). The bigotry of the Emperor, who lived to be eighty-nine, found expression in the lofty, twin-towered mosque that Aurangzib planted high up on the banks of the Ganges in Banaras in order to express his contempt for the Hindu faith. Only one generation after his death the Persian Nadir Shah made his entrance into Delhi, seat of the Mogul Emperors.

Ellora (Plates 77—82)

Just as a European engineer would hardly think of casting a free suspension dome with a span of 143 feet out of cement (without iron reinforcement), so would it appear equally monstrous and impossible to a Western builder to cut a rectangular block of rock out of the side of a mountain using two parallel, perpendicular, longitudinal shafts and a connecting transverse shaft, and then transform this block into a cathedral with lofty, delicate filigree towers, ingenious window and door intrados, columns, pillars, galleries, choirs, balconies, chapels and much statuary. The Indian artist has realised that which the Western artist scarcely dares to dream! He alone had thousands of stone masons at his disposal, sure of themselves and possessing a virtuosity that only a caste heredity thousands of years old can produce. A single false stroke of the chisel at the last moment could have ruined the work of many decades.

The Kailasa temple at Ellora is a vision turned to stone, and although more firmly anchored in the ground than any other temple in the world, it is as near to heaven as the icebound mountain of the gods in the distant Himalayas which gave it its name.

Once Rawana, the tenheaded monster of the deep, attempted to overthrow Siva's throne. With the dreadful strength of his twenty arms spread fan-like he leaned against the walls of his subterranean quarters in order to lift the divine mountain. One statue depicts Parvati, "the maid of the mountains," fearfully clinging to the arm of her husband. But Siva leisurely raises his foot from the couch and places it down on the ground, and the giant strains in vain. Never was the blind rage of crude natural forces and their taming by divine will more convincingly portrayed. The colossal relief itself in the Kailasa temple would be enough to invalidate Goethe's hard criterion of the "wild cave excavations," the "temple of elephants and grimaces" (Zahme Xenien II, Weimar Sophien edition, Vol. 3, p. 257). Goethe knew neither the works of Indian art nor their religious origin; the ban that he imposes on "many-headed gods" does not do justice to the Rawana relief at Ellora nor the statue of the Trinity at Elephanta, which date from about the same time (see Plate 72).

The temple is said to have been built by a certain King Dantidurga, who reigned in the second quarter of the eigth century. But his reign was scarcely long enough to see the completion of the wonder of removing more than 200,000 tons of rock by careful chiseling. The edifice proclaims masterly skill, iron will, and the faith that moves mountains.

Despite its suspended rock bridges, its stirring, dramatic giant reliefs, its bewildering plastic ornament, the Kailasa temple—strangest of all places of worship—rises in clear and distinct outline, as one can see especially well from above (provided one is not prone to dizziness!).

The Indra-Sabha cave was probably built in the eighth century. The "Festive Hall" on the upper floor (see Plate 81) measures fifty-five to sixty-five feet and is supported by twelve pillars that are short and compact, because they have to bear the weight of a whole mountain!

Ajanta (Plates 83-85)

At the northern tip of the former state of Nizam, where the Waghora breaks through the mountains in a semi-circular curve, making foaming waterfalls in the rainy season, lies Ajanta in isolated solitude (Plate 83). As far as I have traveled in the world, I know of no other spot that would be more suited to the preparation of the soul for eternal peace. Here lived those that sought happiness beyond desire, indulgently smiling at those who live in the distant, misty plain and in the daily worry "that my property will not be confiscated by kings, pillaged by robbers, destroyed by fire, washed away by floods or seized by hostile relations." Here lived those who had decided to renounce the world and become monks in self-chosen poverty. A stone bed, a niche for holy books and alms' bowl; that was all. Here they lived as the Master had commanded them, "in learned discussion or holy silence."

The oldest of the twenty-nine caves date back to the year 200 B.C. When Hiuen Tsang visited the place (which was rediscovered only in 1819) in 640 shortly after the death of Mohammed, the only caves that were ever to be finished were completed and in the same condition as we see them today. Seated Buddha statues have a supernatural, magical aspect when the horizontally slanting rays of the setting sun relieve them from the darkness of the shrine in the depths of the cave and kindle the halos to a gentle brightness (Plate 85). Two reclining gazelles indicate the Deer Park where the Master preached for the first time. He turned to all the oppressed, who live down there in the lowlands of life "caught up in a hundred hopes, sunk into greed and anger," as it is expressed in the fourteenth canto of the Bhagavadgita. Hopefully his compassionate words echo from the walls: "The blind shall see again, the deaf always hear, the pregnant shall give birth without pain."

Cave twenty-six, dating from the sixth century, shows the Master in Nirvana (see Plate 10). For the last time Ananda, who, larger than life-size, is to be imagined standing on the right of Plate 84, lays his hands reverently on the Master's feet. Never has human grief found more touching expression than in the pedestal statues. The teacher has already become a god. In the caves of Ajanta one is no longer content with picturesque symbols, as in the Sanchi Stupa. Buddha, the great Indian who preached infinite love to all creatures and thus ethically overcame the caste spirit, is bodily portrayed, not frowning as the Christ of the Byzantines, created in servility and fear (which often scared me in the monastery churches of Ἅγιον ὄρος and the cathedrals of Kiev), but benevolent and redeeming, a forgiving smile on his lips.

We return to the first caves; extravagantly the figures pour forth from wall and ceiling. Beautiful women nestle in the arms of their lovers or lean confidingly on their shoulders, ride in pleasure boats, swing in the swings, full of uninhibited joy and love of life. They are so involved that they do not even honor us late arrivals with so much as a glance! Adjoining, yet only taking up modest space in the total picture, is the birth of Buddha: Maya in her labor clinging to the branches of a salix tree, Boddhi satvas; Buddha's temptation by the evil Mara and his daughters. Then again hunting and courtly scenes; an exotic embassy; bull fights and sea voyages; water birds and lilies; tritons and shells; monkeys and peacocks; a Moorish princess; a shining white, supply-curved feminine nude; an intoxication of color and joy. All these beings surely wish "to live a hundred autumns, rich in possessions, blessed with sons and grandsons" as did their forefathers in Vedic times. We look into open houses, as Giotto painted them eight hundred years later. Costly brocades, sparkling jewelry on splendidly developed figures. An ode to Beauty, as in Sigiriya (Plates 15, 16). Was Buddhism at that time so worldly, so full of the affirmation of life, or do the Ajanta frescos hide some secret that we cannot interpret? Far below in the valley, the waters roar as they roared when the Indian painters conjured up the reflection of a world of beauty and heavenly innocence on the rocky walls.

The Ajanta frescos are of particular importance since we know practically nothing of the thousand years that separate them from the Persian-influenced, courtly miniatures of the Mogul era in Indian painting.

Dabhoi (Plate 88)

Dabhoi lies in the former territory of the Gaekwar of Baroda, whose state has a certain similarity to pre-war Thuringia by reason of its enclaves. With its well preserved, early-medieval walls and gates the little town vividly recalls Rothenburg ob der

Tauber. The Hira Gate, situated on the east side of the ramparts, is 36¹/₂ feet high. "Adam and Eve," near whom on the left a devil is lying in wait, measure about four feet. (For "maiden and tree" motif see p. 22.)

Champaner (Plates 86, 87)

In Champaner too mighty ramparts remain undamaged. The ancient Rajputan fortress fell in 1484 to Mahmud Bigara of Ahmadabad; in 1535 it was stormed by the Emperor Humayun, who with a small, picked force scaled the walls himself by means of iron hooks and personally opened the gates of the town to his troops. Besides the dignified restored Great Mosque and the Borah Masjid, there are countless mosques, minarets, palaces and fountains scattered in the surrounding forests which testify to a glorious past.

Ahmadabad (Plates 21, 22, 89-92)

If Daboi is the Indian Rothenburg, then Ahmadabad, the capital of Gujarat on the Sabarmati, is the Indian Augsburg. The ancient merchant families of Jaina could compare with the wealth of the Fuggers and Welsers; their home town with the imperial residences on the Jumna. In 1615, when Thomas Roe was in India, Ahmadabad was as large as contemporary London. Founded by Sultan Ahmad I in 1411, it flourished for a hundred years. Then followed a period of decline. When in 1573 Ahmadabad fell into the hands of Akbar, it prospered anew. Its splendor disappeared together with the Moguls. Under British rule the town received a fresh impetus. Today it has a population of nearly a million, and its cotton trade is world famous.

No chronicle tells so impressively of fame and wealth as do buildings. Fifteen cupolas arch over the Jami-Masjid, which contains 260 tall, slender columns inside. Bijapur favored spacious, clear interiors; Ahmadabad prefers charming, ever-changing prospects of Kiblas and raised galleries. One seems to be walking through a tall-stemmed palm grove. The mosque of Muhafiz Khan also dates from the earliest period of prosperity. One of the most graceful mosque gates in Bijapur is called Mihtari Mahal because it was built by a poor water-carrier, who unexpectedly acquired great wealth and could think of no better use for it than to build a worthy entrance to the mosque. In Ahmadabad we owe a charming little work of art—the Sidi Saiyad mosque—to a slave (of Ahmad Shahs I).

The marble window in Plate 92 is of a nobility far above human words. Whoever has stood in the interior of the mosque when the golden afternoon sun outlines the splendid creeper pattern on the marble floor like a carpet whose patterns and coloring change continually will silently take leave of Ahmad's city—happy and purified.

Girnar (Plates 107, 108)

If, of twelve colored plates, two are devoted to one sacred place, then Indian art must find its most noble expression in this sanctified spot, and Indian spirit its deepest revelation. Personal considerations also play a part. As the brown tide rose ever higher in my homeland and drove me from desk and lecture hall, I found refuge on these heights; and here, in out-of-the-world solitude, as guest of the Jain brotherhood, nearly twenty years later, I experienced on the day of Our Lord's Birth that night of consecration which even the divinely favored experiences only once in his earthly lifetime.

The mountain, 3580 feet high, already a place of pilgrimage before Asoka's time, is dedicated to Nemnath, the 22nd Tirthankar (Preparer of the way, Ford-finder) of the Jaina, to whom the brothers Tejapala and Vastupala have erected a magnificent temple on Mount Abu. The great triplet temple that the brothers built on Girnar in 1177 immediately behind the Nemnath temple is dedicated to Mallinath, the 19th Tirthankar, and contains his image.

Whoever comes from the holy mountain of Girnar going towards the town of Junagadh shortly before reaching the old fortress of Uparkot becomes aware of a hall-like building, which a huge, unhewn granite rock is supposed to protect from the weather. Mankind would have been spared much suffering if their rulers had adopted the high political morals which Chandragupta's famous grandson Asoka entrusted to stone as a pattern for his own dealings and as a legacy to his successors here, in Kalsi and in Jaugada: "Once kings used to make pleasure journeys where there were hunts and other such pastimes. But when the beloved of the gods, King Piyadasi (Asoka) had been anointed ten years, he went to Sambodhi (Buddh Gaya). And he undertook such journeys for religious reasons, to visit Brahmins and ascetics and to bring them gifts, to visit the aged and support them with gold, to visit the people in the provinces and to instruct them in religion and to question them about religion as a means thereto. That was a far greater pleasure for the beloved of the gods, King Piyadasi." Thus runs Asoka's rock edict in Girnar (Winternitz' translation). The Kalsi stone on the Jumna, not far from Dehra Dun, warns sons and grandsons against warlike conquests; they should regard only religious conquests as true conquests. In Jaugada, Asoka addresses himself to his immediate neighbors, and this edict is perhaps the most beautiful legacy that ever a ruler left: "All men are my children. And just as I desire happiness and well-being for my children in this world and the next, so I desire the same for all men. It could be that my frontier neighbors think, 'what are the King's intentions towards us?' Only this wish on their behalf should reach them: the King wishes that they should not be afraid of him. They should trust in me, and they shall receive joy, not suffering, at my hands." These splendid words, in which for the first time in history, a ruler of a large kingdom clearly proclaims the ideal of humanity, ring like a warning reproach in our age, where the relations of nations, despite the well-sounding phrases uttered by their airborne Heads of State chasing from conference to conference and from party to party, are still founded on fear and distrust.

That Asoka's rock and column edicts were not only graven in stone, but also practised, is proved by the friendly relations of the Maurya kings with the Egyptian Ptolemies and the Syrian Seleucids. Perhaps it is not by chance that Manu's codex, that claims supernatural origins, dates from the time immediately after Asoka. Gambling and betting—passions which the modern state not only tolerates but even furthers because it derives gain from them—gambling and betting were put on an equal basis with theft and the authorities ordered not to tolerate them. This is evidence of an ethical feeling which we have completely lost or which we never possessed.

Satrunjaya (Plate 113)

Many thousands of miles lie between the sea-washed peninsula Kathiawar and Northern France. And yet a straight line connects the bastion-like corner towers of the sacred mount Satrunjaya, in the state of Saurashtra, to the Gothic cathedrals of the West.

A kindly fate enabled us on the day of departure from Ahmadabad to attend a colorful procession on the occasion of an annual feast of the Jain community (see Plate 21).

Long and hot is the railway journey from Ahmad's city to Palitana, hot and desert-like the countryside surrounding the temple city on the mountains. At the foot of the mountain a dholi—sedan chair—carried by four porters awaits me, but I prefer to go on foot like a pilgrim in thin, linen sandals given me so that the mountain, which pilgrims only tread barefoot, should not be desecrated by my leather shoes. Although the sun burns pitilessly, I reverently remove my topee. The aged temple guardian, who recognises me despite the many intervening years, answers the outer sign of my respect by binding a linen cloth about my head and hot temples as protection against the scorching sun. After refreshing myself with a little fruit and a gulp of tea (meat, fish, eggs and vegetables grown under the soil are forbidden Jain believers by religious rule), I look straight down from the balcony of the pilgrims' hostel into the deep, green, overgrown cistern, from which the water is still drawn in bags as in days long ago. Then, as deeply moved as formerly, I look across from the rest-house gallery to the countless shrines gleaming in the sunlight.

Two peaks are separated by a pass, and each bears a self-contained, defense-walled enclosure of temples. The holy city is not inhabited by men. Only gods live here, close to the heavens—in more than eight hundred temples. Its foundation goes back to the eleventh century. The holy mountain has experienced troubled times too when the Moslems entered the land in the fourteenth and fifteenth centuries. But since then, peace has reigned in the temple city on the mountain heights—devout stillness, that is broken only now and then by the peal of a bell, the chant of pious pilgrims or the wing beats of tame doves that nest here in the thousands, under the protection of the gods on the mountain of peace.

Dwarka (Plate 98)

Again the solitude of the dunes surrounds us. Dwarka is one of the seven great places of pilgrimage of India and is dedicated to Krishna, here worshipped as "Dwarkanath." His immense temple is said to have grown up in a single night. Mira Bai, a princess of Jodhpur, venerated the god especially fervently in song: "I have left land and treasures and am no longer a queen. Fleeing to thee as thy slave comes Mira Bai. O take her to thee." Thereupon the stone image of the god opened and he took her to himself for ever. The last rays of the setting sun gild the temple on the beach. "I am not revealed to everyone," says Krishna in the Song of the Sublime, "because the Maya splendor hides me." Yet Arjuna, his charioteer, saw him as "the eternal source of all being":

"Thou art the eternal protector of eternal right,
As the eternal original spirit do I comprehend
thee . . ."

And the surge of the waves sounds like the presence of a personal god.

The Bhagavadgita which has Krishna as its central figure, praised by Wilhelm von Humboldt as "the profoundest and noblest that the world has to offer," is one of the few poetical works by Indian priestly bards that is completely theist in thought. "I am immortality and death," says Krishna to his charioteer. "I am existence, and I am non-existence, Arjuna . . ." "Do thy duty; do not ask after success of thy actions. Never let success of thy actions be the reason for thy work!"—thoughts of the Königsberg sage, but uttered two thousand years before him!

Jamnagar (Plate 93)

The former reigning royal house is of Rajputan blood. The family origin reveals itself in many buildings and in the energy with which each work was begun and carried through. Marble quarries, copper mines and pearl fishing on the southern shore of the Gulf of Cutch bring the small state considerable income for cultural expenditure.

Moodhera (Plates 96, 99, 100)

Moodhera lies, like Dabhoi, in the former Gaekwar state. Its temples belong roughly to the same time as the city ramparts of Dabhoi (c. 1100 according to the estimate of Ananda Coomaraswamy).

Vadnagar (Plate 101)

One seldom finds in such a small Indian town so many intellectual faces as here. Vadnagar is the center of the Nagar-Brahmins, whose influence is great in all Gujarat and on the peninsula of Kathiawar.

Kheda (Plate 102)

Kheda lies in Cutch, the largest of the 189 formerly independent Kathiawar states. The "Runn" which surrounds the state to the north and southeast (see map) has the appearance of our shoals, magnified to gigantic proportions. At the time of the southwest monsoons, Cutch is a large, sea-washed island. In the dry season one can ride over the endless hard, dried-mud desert, which because of its salt content produces no spark of life—neither animal nor vegetable. Kheda lies about twelve miles south of the capital, Bhuj. Its Siva temple dates from the tenth century.

Sidhpur (Plate 114)

The town on the Sarasvati, belonging to the ancient kingdom of Baroda, traces its foundation back to 950. The Rudra Mala temple, built of cyclopic stone blocks, was destroyed in 1297 by Ala-ud-din Khilji.

Mount Abu (Plates 104, 109)

Stone garlands swing from column to column, which themselves have shaken off all earthly weight and have broken up in filigree. Where the flat dome begins numerous figures from Jain legend are enthroned on the delicate corbels and also dance their round among the shafts of the columns. The keystone is formed into a cone-shaped, hanging blossom that puts even the noblest Gothic creations into the shade. Everything in the temple, dedicated to Adinath, the first Tirthankar (Ford-finder) of the Jains, is executed with the same care—the numerous chapels, in which sit marble Tirthankaras with sparkling crystal eyes, every single coffer of the ceiling in the side aisle, each one different from the others (Plate 109). Inexhaustible was the imagination of the unknown artists. All technical difficulties are playfully overcome; both figures and ornament are so deeply graven that doves can nest behind the marble work without being seen. Only their cooing betrays them. The Jain brotherhood that is as old as the Buddhist did not like to hew monuments out of rock. They are situated free on the mountains, often united in veritable temple cities, as on the Girnar and Satrunjaya peaks, with a magnificent view of the far countryside; inside however, they are fairy castles which still put all who enter them into a fairy-tale mood.

The much mentioned Jains today form a community of about a million believers—as opposed to a hundred million Moslems unevenly spread over the whole peninsula, and to more than three hundred million Hindus. In the past also their strength seems to have been unrelated to the costly temples and monuments that they have left behind them. Fifteen hundred years ago India forged a fully corrosion-free iron column fourteen inches in diameter and thirty-one feet long (it stands beside the Kutb Minar in Delhi); India dragged gigantic blocks of marble from quarries almost two hundred miles away up to the 3900 foot high Mount Abu and shaped them there as if they were wax! "There is only one India! It is the only country that has a monopoly of grand and imposing specialities. Its marvels are its own. The patents cannot be infringed; imitations are not possible!" Those are not the words of an enthusiastic European art historian, but those of an American, Mark Twain, who brought nothing else to India than the most valuable heritage of his people, a keen power of observation and common-sense.

The three buffalo (reproduced on Plate 104, confronted by the graceful little dancer), look out over a small pond which nowadays contains little water. Once this pond was filled with a ghi (purefied butter for religious purposes, see p. 18 and Plate 42). The three buffalo came every night and drank from this holy oil until the arrow of the Pramara king Adi Pal killed all three at once and turned them into stone. One can still see clearly the hole made by the arrowshot.

Ranapur (Plates 110, 115)

The narrow track railway which runs northwards from Abu Road stops after a three-hour night journey in Falna. There is no waiting-room, not even the most modest form of accomodation, and the fever shakes me and the diarrhetic colic racks me. I had let myself be persuaded to eat a "European dinner" at Abu Road Station that was apparently made from spoiled tinned meat. Adjoining the tiny station office is a small lumber-room. Here I spent the night shivering. As there was no doctor anywhere in the vicinity I had no alternative but to continue in a rickety bus to Sadri, and from there, in a still more rickety bus that I had to charter myself, to Ranapur (Rampura). A friendly old man, guardian of the temple and of age-old wisdom, to whom I had handed my recommendations and told of my plight, advised me to forego all food that day, and on the next, to eat only a handful of boiled rice. I too had smiled at the fasting of Indian ascetics and the Sadhu hunger cures. Now I fasted myself, refused the refractory stomach all nourishment and was well again on the third day! Perhaps also the mental side aided in the recovery—an iron will and enthusiasm.

Admiringly, the eye moves from cornice to cornice, from one arabesque to another, from figure to figure until it comes to rest on the selfcontained roundness of the cupola. As a young student I had looked up to the zenith of the dome which Master Sinan, the greatest Turkish architect, had arched in the mosque of Sultan Selim in Adrianople. It pales by comparison with the creation of the unknown Indian master of Ranapur, commissioned by Kumbha, Rana of Udaipur, who worked 130 years before him.

Shyly, I stare up at the low suspended keystone of the arch. Here the Gothic spirit has found its final, most convincing expression. Everything that I saw on this plane in the Western world becomes null and meaningless. In the Great Temple of Ranapur the spirit celebrates its finest triumph over the material. The anonymous master of Ranapur had dedicated himself completely to them; and the gods, who live in the mountain temples all around in the land of the Jains, blessed him, winged his imagination, and guided his chisel so that he breathed a soul into the insensitive marble and was able to transform obstinate stone into graceful dreams.

Now I already wander for days along the galleries and amidst the forest of richly carved, slender columns. Again and again I discover new hidden beauties. The bitter hour of departure approaches. In the depths of the hall still brood the bluish shadows of the night. Then the first ray of the rising sun triumphantly catches the crystal lamp that swings above the image of a holy elephant. And the place is filled with a magic light whose shine is no longer of this world, but quite, quite transcendental!

Ajmer (Plate 97)

Ajmer is farther into Rajasthan—"the land of kings' sons," as the warlike inhabitants call themselves, and with justified pride. In 1536 the great Akbar laid his hands on the strategically important Ajmer and annually he pilgrimaged to the tomb of Khwaja

Muin-ud-din Chisthis [who died in 633 of the Hegira (1255)]. He still did so in ripe old age, and the annals report that the aged Emperor made many of his pilgrimages from Agra or the distant Fatehpur Sikri to Ajmer on foot in order to show particular respect for the saint who became the ancestor of a proud race of intellectual leaders of his people. Up to the present day the sacred enclosure of the Dargah, shaded by ancient trees, attracts crowds of pilgrims. At particularly festive occasions, they are fed from the great bronze pot that holds no less than ten tons of rice.

Solitary, half sunk into the swamp, under an old forsaken tree, stands a small stone pillar. Seldom does someone err into Umarkot, that borders on to the province of "King's sons" and now belongs to Pakistan, for it is sparsely populated and bare. When Humayun, a contemporary of Charles V, had to flee before his adversary, the Afghan Shah, he guided his footsteps into this desert and here, where under decaying arch the modest stone mourns, his son was born. As Emperor his son was to fill the world with his fame—Akbar, "the Great," the "King of kings," the "Shadow of God." The great Emperor could neither read nor write but gladly listened to the words of philosophers and poets (see p. 15). Like the magnificent Alexander before him, he sought to amalgamate the different elements of his large Empire into a unified whole, a settlement between Moslem and Hindu. Already Kabir, who was born a century before Akbar as the child of a Brahmin widow and educated by a Mohammedan weaver, had striven for this settlement and for an intensification of Islam, which was threatening to lose its best qualities in warfare.

"Why Mullah, must you ascend the minaret?
God is not deaf, He hears thee here.
For His sake do you call to prayer:
Look for Him in thy heart, so says Kabir!"

Amber (Plate 94)

The proud ancient royal seat, only five miles from Jaipur, the contemporary capital of Rajasthan, was founded in 928—exactly 800 years before Jaipur. Its pride is the palace, reflected in a lake, which can be considered the finest monument of Rajputan architecture. Just now the morning sun shines through the veil-like, patterned alabaster windows in the loggia of the wing of the palace reserved for the women. And the view of the lake in the valley is as beautiful as the windows. The low position of the small, hand-operated wing of the windows is explained by the Oriental custom of sitting on the floor.

Mandu (Plate 116)

The nearest railway station is fifty-five miles away, and only a secondary train stops there. The kingdom of the Moslem Malwa kings has fallen, but their tombs and mosques still remain, scattered over an area of thirty-six miles.

The rays of the morning sun intrude far into the Jami Masjid or Great Mosque, which opens wide to the East. Under its kiss of fire the stone awakens to mysterious life. Its color changes from old ivory to bronze-gold and blood-red according to the veins of the stone and the position of the sun. The old craftsman wisely abstained from all decoration.

Mysterious lurks the jungle, ready to reembrace in its inescapable arms that which it has kept hidden for centuries. For days I wander through the ruins on the constant lookout for poisonous creatures in swamp and grass around stubborn, defensive walls, often slightly escarped, as on a fortress and weighty, heavy cupolas, as if built for eternity. "If an arch entrusts itself to the keystone, then it is surely built for eternity." (The Emperor to the Chancellor-Archbishop in *Faust, Part II*, by Goethe.)

From one of these tomb cupolas an echo answers me, gently fading as if angelic voices were calling from the far distance of Paradise. Enchanted, I look up to the undecorated dome, where the last light of day is fading. Why did you take your acoustic secret with you into the grave, you great unknown master? Darkness falls. The mosquitoes begin to hum. Perhaps it was *they* that drove the active men from their huts and palaces. Eerily night comes creeping from the jungle—a night that is no friend to man. When, a few minutes later in a fragile, habitable ruin I was making up my bed, a soul-searing cry of a wild beast or its victim pierced the wild, primeval solitude. In Mandu the law of the jungle is respected—the merciless right of the stronger. And the jungle was stronger than the mighty Malwa kings!

Long and hot is our journey to the valley of the Indus. Whirling sand, now and then at long intervals a wretched hamlet, a few camels that stretch their necks and foam furiously when suddenly the giant metal bird roars over them, linking Djakarta with Amsterdam, and London with Australia and New Zealand—fifteen thousand miles of flight! We too gaze surprised after the four-engined monster. Yet in our admiration for the achievements of modern technic, we should not forget the great deeds of the past. In Akbar's day—whose reign of fifty years forms a height of Indian development and one of the happiest chapters in the history of mankind— there was a state post that accomplished the immense distance from the lower Indus to Delhi in five days!

Hyderabad-Sind (Plate 106)

Hyderabad-Sind is a comparatively new town. It was founded in 1768 as capital of the united Sind by Ghulam Shah Kalhora. The reader looks from the fort onto the town, in whose houses a summer temperature of 110—120° Fahrenheit is not at all unusual!

Tatta (Plates 111, 112)

It is the year 711. The Near East and North Africa have been won over to Islam; Tarik, the Caliph's general, crosses the straits that still bear his name and destroys the Visigothic kingdom at Xeres in Spain. Despite the enormous forces of the West, the young Islam feels strong enough to push forward also in the East. En route from Ceylon to Iraq, a fleet carrying costly pearls and Mecca pilgrims is plundered by pirates, whose hideout is on the Sind coast. On Friday, the 10th Muharram in the year 93 of the Hegira (711), a Moslem army appears before Debal, the modern Tatta. Over the Hindu temple floats the green silk flag as a landmark. The commander of the army, who is only seventeen years old, gives the commanding officer of artillery, Jaubat Salmi, the order to shoot the flag down. Ten thousand diram is the reward. Should he fail, he is to lose both hands. Five hundred strong arms tighten the string of their mighty catapult and to the cry of "Allah is mighty, Allah is mighty," the banner sinks

to the ground. Seven hundred beautiful Devadases are captured as slaves in the temple. Two daughters of the king Dahir are also captured and sent as booty to the Caliph. In order to revenge themselves on the general who had brought such misfortune on their house, the maidens declare that Muhammad ibn Kasim has already dishonored them and the young Arab commander is cruelly executed. When it is later discovered that the maidens had lied, they are subjected to an even more painful death.—The conquest of Sind is a drama worthy of a Shakespeare. The Emir of Sind, with whom the Emperor Humayun found refuge, was Mirza Shah Hasan (see p. 32). His successor, Mirza Isa Khan, died in 1644 at the age of ninety-two. His long life enabled him to erect a real jewel casket as a mausoleum. The embossed worked arabesques of ivory sandstone can compete with Akbar's castle at Fatehpur Sikri. Also the enclosure of his wives' tombs is a place of great solemnity, carefully sculptured outside as well as inside (Plate 112). Even one who is not given to superlatives will agree with Migeon, the great expert on Islamic Art: "There is no art that offers more decorative wealth and sovereign harmony." Today it is forty-eight miles to Karachi; at the time of Muhammad ibn Kasim one saw the sea from this hill. Tatta has wandered inland, like the ancient cities on the lower Irrawaddy.

Between the conquest of Sind by the Mohammedans and the building of its Emirs shown here passed nine centuries—of which we know practically nothing. To be situated in the lower valley of the Indus is perilous since, dammed by tidal current, its waters often seek a new bed. Thus the river completely reshaped the landscape round Hyderabad as recently as 1758. The Mohammedans have never found it beneath their dignity to have their places of worship built by unbelievers. The Great Mosque at Ahmadabad reveals a charming amalgamation of Moslem planning and Hindu craftsmanship. The oldest, well-preserved funereal monument in Tatta, that of Nizam-u-din (Jan-Nindo), who ruled Sind from 1461 to 1509 and raised her to great power, is especially elucidating to art historians. It reveals the Moslem employer in conflict with the employed

Hindu craftsmen, a conflict which lasted two centuries. Our reproduction shows the result. The face of the new-found style is shown in especially expressive examples that we have contrasted on Plates 111 and 112, not without artistic intention (as the bulls of Achilgarh and the charming little dancer in Plates 103 and 104).

Mohenjo Daro (Plate 103)

Here we see well planned canalization, which would rouse the envy of many a European mayor; bath installations that satisfy the extensive requirements of modern hygiene; little clay figures with movable heads as toys; detailedly formed seals showing keenly-observed animals; choice feminine jewelry; the natural chalk bust of a bearded man in richly ornamented robe; the bronze statuette of a bejeweled, over-slim dancing girl with sensually parted lips. Modern man stands a little shame-faced before the treasures that have come to light in Mohenjo Daro. The progress we have made in five milleniums is slight, very modest indeed, after such promising beginnings! That in the last thirty years we can look back to a time that is older than the Vedic hymns, a time which no monument had revealed to us until then, we owe solely to the preserving earth of Sind and to the English archæologist, Sir John Marshall (1902—31).

It is not the purpose of this book to examine the implications of the finds that lay buried deep under Buddhist ruins, i.e. how far the pre-Aryan culture and civilization of the Indus valley is related to the Sumerian, old Babylonian, etc. The Archæological Camp Office was kind enough to release the irre-placable bronze statuette from its treasures. In the museum garden the young girl was again allowed to drink in the long-missed sunlight, and her enchanted eyes opened wide. May the reader rightly understand the words which the hyper-delicate little dancer calls to him across the span of five thousand years: "Come to India and be amazed!"

Kandahar (Plate 105)

People of Kandahar "Gandarioi" are already mentioned among the mercenaries that Xerxes led against the Greeks. Even in those years they must have been brave warriors, like the Gurkhas from the mountains of Nepal. "A Mohammedan from Delhi is worth ten Hindus, but one from the frontier is worth one hundred." Every British officer and soldier who has once served at the most dangerous frontier of the Empire—in Northwest India—can tell a tale or two about that. Shortly beyond the village of Chaman, to which the former British military railway winds its way in mighty bends, is the frontier. Gun muzzles gleam; dignified, white-bearded patriarchs are gathered around with grunting water-pipes—Afghanistan. The men are still vigorous and elastic at seventy: "A breeze from the mountains blows twenty years away from a man's age."

We have traveled swiftly over thousands of years and wandered thousands of miles. We saw nations come and go like the clay buckets of an Indian well, that rises out of the depths of the earth and sinks again into the bosom of the earth. But as the clay bucket with the drawn water fertilizes the land, so all these races have enriched the ground of Asia with the creations of their spirit. Works of literature are difficult to grasp in their beauty. Translations are like the inside of a knitted garment; they show the pattern, but never the beauty. Plastic works of art speak directly, need no interpreter.
The last step of the eightfold way to bliss is called by Asia's greatest son, who attained the highest peak of human understanding, the right Absorption. May the reader put away the unrest of the white man and become absorbed in that which the best of many nations and many centuries have created for him also!

Siva Nataraja (Plate 117)

He whirls in a dance, which projects the Earth through the universe, the braided strands of hair swinging around the god's three-eyed head. The hair forms a high crown, in the left of which gleams the sickle moon. Strands of hair, doubled arms proclaiming omnipotence, dangling snakes and legs that tread on the dark powers of the deep form the spokes of the flaming wheel of the sun. Siva unites male and female in one person, as is revealed by his ears: the long, hanging right one, the ring-ornamented one on the left. The lower (foreground) left hand directs the worshipper to the god's foot where he can seek refuge; the lower right hand is raised in blessing. The upper right hand holds a small drum, for vibration comes at the beginning of every event. The upper left holds a flame—profound symbol for destruction and purification. And purifying tongues of flame lick all around the edges of the shining disc of the sun, which serves as the god's halo.

The reader may well ask himself if he knows a work of art in which beginning and end are so convincingly portrayed in cosmic size. The artist who cast this bronze was near to the gods. With this work we will take leave of our original home —Asia—with grateful hearts.

We came and shall go; even the works that we have looked at will perish; but the artistic idea will remain eternally, and eternally, Siva will dance the Tandava, unconcerned by us tiny men, untroubled by life and death!

PLATES

1. Praying before the "Golden" Pagoda in Rangoon

2. Pagan, Thatbyinnyu (erected about 1100)

3. Pagan, Maha-Bodhi Pagoda

4. Giant Buddha of Pegu. The original form dates from the year 994.

5. Amarapura, Dragon Pagoda

6. Sagaing, the massive Kaunghmudaw, erected in 1636

7. Mandalay, the Queen's (Supaya Lat) Golden Monastery

8. View from the Mihintale Rock, where King Tissa of Ceylon received Asoka's son and first missionary of Buddhism

9. Polonnaruwa, Round Temple Wata Dagé

10. Polonnaruwa, Gal Vihara: Buddha in the Nirvana; at his head his favorite diciple, Ananda.

11. Rock statue at Polonnaruwa, for a long time thought to represent King Parakrama the Great (12th century)

12. Gods at foot of the rock monastery Isurumuniya near Anuradhapura

13. Dwarpal on the flight of steps ascending to the Thuparama Dagoba at Anuradhapura, the oldest pagoda
in Ceylon

14. Rock fortress Sigiriya, refuge of King Kasyapa, the parricide, about 500 A.D.

15. The famous Sigiriya frescoes

16. Sigiriya, a graceful girl, lavishly adorned with jewelry, painted *al fresco*, in deep, unbroken colors

17. Anuradhapura, so-called Moonstone (in the main frieze a procession of lions, horses, elephants, and humpbacked oxen)

18. A group, stained in vived colors, in a gateway of the Temple of Rameswaram

19. Dancing Śiva in the interior of the Great Temple of Madura (*cf.* No. 117)

20. Madurai, palace of Tirumala Nayak, the founder of the Great Temple

21. A Jain procession taking place during a Temple feast in Ahmadabad

22. A Moslem teacher with his pupils in the Rani Sipri Mosque at Ahmadabad

23. Pottery horses of the god Ayyanar for his nightly rides around the boundaries of the village (*cf.* No. 27)

24. The unfinished mountain temple of Kalugumalai

25. Madurai, the upper stories of the South-Gopuram of the Great Temple

26. Village deities at Thiruwanaikawal (near Trichinopoly), stained with glaring paint

27. Horses and elephants, mounts of the rural god Ayyanar (Kolanelli near Erode, District of Karur; *cf.* No. 23)

28. Sri Rangam, chariot of the god, drawn by the faithful, at the time of the great festivals, with the aid of ropes

29. Kumbakonam, Sarangapani (Vishnu) Temple with eleven-story gate-tower

30. Chidambaram, Siva Temple, a jewel of Dravidian art

31. Mahabalipuram, or Mamallapuram, seashore temple (8th century; *cf.* No. 98)

32. Two of the so-called "Seven Pagodas" of Mahabalipuram, which were chiseled collectively out of the rising rock (*cf.* Nos. 40, 41)

33. Pillars in the Kaliana mandapam of the Temple of Vellore

34. Nandi on Chamundi Hill, two miles southeast of Mysore (*cf*. No. 49)

35. Tiruvannamalai, one of the few Hindu temples whose entire structure may be seen from a single viewpoint

36. Seringapatam, snake idols beneath a banyan tree. In the background, the water gate in defense of which Tipu Sultan lost his life.

37. Jakanacharya's masterpiece: the temple of Somnathpur (*cf.* No. 48)

38. Halebid, Hoysaleswara Temple, a worthy counterpart of the temple of Somnathpur (*cf.* Nos. 37, 39)

39. Base of the temple of Somnathpur (*cf.* No. 37)

40. Bas-relief of the so-called "Penance of Arjuna," 90′ long and 30′ high

41. Combat between Siva's consort Durga and the buffalo-headed demon. Mahishamardini mandapam (Mahabalipuram).

42. Belgola of the Sravans (Jains), early colossal statue of a sage. Clinging vines symbolize his profound meditation.

43. Chapel on the slope of Mount Indrabetta, on the summit of which rises the statue presented on the left

44. Halebid, interior of the Hoysaleswara (No. 38), passage linking the twin temples

45. Ganesa, Siva's son, the elephant-headed God of Wisdom, in front of the Hoysaleswara Temple at Halebid

47. Vijayanagar, granite formation, which offered the artist only rugged material
(cf. No. 60)

46. Pattadakal, temple in north Indian style, vertical lines

48. Main temple of Belur, erected in the reign of the Hoysala-King Vishnu Vardhana, early 12th century, built by Jakanacharya (cf. No. 37)

49. Lakkandi, where Siva was held in special reverence as Nandeswar, "Lord of the Bull Nandi" (*cf.* No. 34)

50. Vijayanagar, Ganesh temple. Without the tower in the background, it would resemble a Greek temple.

51. Pillar in the Kashi-Vishwanath Temple at Lakkandi. The black-green polished stone and the minute craftmanship are reminiscent of bronze (*cf.* No. 63).

53. Vijayanagar, "City of Victory," corner tower of the Zenana- (Harem-) District, Indo-Saracen style

52. Vijayanagar, capital city, from 1336–1565, of the mighty kingdom of the same name. Snake deity.

54. Badami (ancient capital of the Chalukyas), Brahman rock temple, second half of 6th century

55. Vijayanagar, base of throne-hall

56. Aiholi (eight miles northeast of Pattadakal), Durga Temple (*cf.* No. 46)

57. Supports in the Hindu fortress of Warangal, taken by storm in 1323 by the Mohammedans under Tughlaq (*cf.* No. 66)

58. Sati-Stones (memorials to cremated widows) at Vijayanagar

59. Vijayanagar, temple of Vithoba, an incarnation of Vishnu

60. Vijayanagar, gigantic image of the Narsingh Avatar (Vishnu in his incarnation as a man-lion), carved out of a single
block of granite

61. Stone chariot in the court of the Vithoba or Vijaya Vitalaswami Temple (*cf.* No. 28)

62. Gate sculpture in the temple of Rameswaraswami at Tadpatri (founded in 1485 by the Vijayanagar dynasty). Ancient Indian decorative motif.

63. Palampet, temple on Ramappa Lake. "The brightest star in the galaxy of medieval Deccan temples" (Gulam Yazdani) (*cf*. No. 51).

65. Afzalganj Masjid at Hyderabad, another building displaying four towers

64. Hyderabad, Deccan, the "Char Minar" as seen from the court of the Mecca Mosque

66. Warangal, one of the four state-gates which are reminiscent of wood work (*cf.* Nos. 57, 58)

67. The mausoleum of Muhammed 'Adil Shah of Bijapur, called the Gol Gumbaz or "Round Dome," which spans 30' wider than the dome of St. Paul's

68. Bijapur, one of the marble windows with verse from the Koran, of the Ibrahim Rauza, the tomb of 'Adil Shah and his consort (*cf.* No. 92)

69. Bijapur, road-gate with superstructure. Keel-shaped, wedge-cut arch.

70. Aurangabad, Mecca gate and bridge

71. Gulbarga, fantastic gateway in the burial quarter of Banda Nawaz

72. Indian girls in native costume before the "Trinity" in the excavated temple of Elephanta Island

73. Royal donors in front of the Chaitya of Karli, the woman lavishly ornamented with a wide girdle, heavy ankle and arm-bracelets

74. Buddhist rock temple at Karli—ante Christian era (dimensions: 124′ 3″ in length; 45′ in breadth; 46′ in height)

75. Cave temple at Kondane, distinctly reminiscent of ancient wooden structures (*cf.* No. 66)

76. Kanheri, stone enclosure in front of Cave No. 3, clearly a translation from architecture in wood

77. Elephants hewn, as is the entire temple, from live rock support the main shrine of the Kailasa Temple (No. 79).

78. The Kailasa Temple at Ellora, named after Śiva's mountain castle in the Himalayas, 8th century (108' high, covering a surface of 154' × 276')

79. Crowning roof of the elephant-supported main shrine (photographed from a point on the upper right of No. 78, at the edge of the precipice)

80. Sunrise in the outer court of the Indra Sabha Cave at Ellora dedicated to the Jain cult

81. "Indra's Festival Hall," loggia on the upper floor. The god mounted on his sacred elephant.

82. Ellora, Rameswara Cave, dedicated to Siva. The Nandi-Bull in front of the temple is also hewn from live rock (cf. No. 34).

83. Ajanta, partial view of the semicircle of temples cut into the mountainside

84. Buddha in the Nirvana, with mourners at the base. Gigantic piece of sculpture in the left side-aisle of Cave No. 26.

85. Teaching Buddha. Gigantic statue at Ajanta, Cave No. 16

86. The Jami Masjid in the ancient Rajput fortress of Champaner (capital of Mahmud Bigara of Ahmadabad since 1484)

87. Champaner, Borah Masjid

88. Oriel on the Hira Gate at Dabhoi (Baroda State). 12th century(?)

89. Ahmadabad, Jami Masjid, built by Sultan Ahamad I. in 1424. In the background the gallery for the royal wives.

90. Prayer niche and lampstand in the mosque which was built in 1465 by Jamal-ud-din Muhafiz Khan, subsequently governor of Ahmadabad

91. Ornamental niche in the entrance-wall of the Great Mosque of Ahmadabad

92. Ahmadabad, marble window of the Sidi Saiyad (*cf.* No. 68)

93. Zenana (Harem) of the old palace of Jamnagar

94. Harem windows in the palace at Amber (begun 1600 by Man Singh)

95. Sinnar (twenty miles south of Nasik), Gondesvara Temple

96. Moodhera (territory of H.H. the Gaekwar of Baroda), temple of the sun-god, Suriya

97. One of the holiest goals of the pilgrims of Islam: the burial place of Khwaja Muin-ud-din Chishti
(died 1235) in Ajmer

98. Temple on the beach of Dwarka in the rays of the setting sun

99. A glimpse of the detached pillar, seen from the interior of the temple in No. 96

100. The temple of Moodhera with terraces on the Pond of Atonement, pawed up, according to legend, by the steeds of the sun-god

101. Kirti Stambha of Vadnagar

102. Temple at Kheda (Cutch Peninsula)

103. Mohenjo Daro, bronze statuette of a dancer (4¹⁄₄″ high), the earliest Indian woman known to us, 3rd millennium B.C.

104. Gigantic bulls on the road from the Dilwara temples, Mount Abu (*cf.* No. 109) to Achilgarh

105. View of Kandahar, the city wall and the distant mountains

106. Hyderabad Sind, one of the hottest towns in India, with windscreens on the flat roofs

107. Mountain chapel on the pilgrim's path to Girnar

108. View of the mountain temple at Girnar and the magnificent landscape about it

109. Marble ceiling in the Vimala Temple, Mount Abu (completed in the year 1031, when Kaiser Konrad II. laid the foundation stone for the cathedral of Speyer)

110. In the great Jain Temple of Ranapur, carved of the finest marble by an unknown master

111. Tatta, detail of the mausoleum of Nawab Isa Khan

112. Prayer niche in the wall enclosing the tombs of the wives of Nawab Isa Khan

113. View of the sun-baked plain from the Himalayan peak, Satrunjaya

114. Sidhpur, ruins of the Rudra Mala Temple (destroyed by Ala-ud-din Khilji in 1297)

115. Under the vast domes of the Ranapur temple are found God's peace and security

116. Mandu. Cracked arches, swamps, mosquitoes, malaria—that is all that remains of the mighty wealth of the Malwa kings!

117. Dancing Siva in a ring of flames. Precious bronze from Kankoduttavanitham, Tanjore District (Museum at Madras).

One hundred eighteen plates, black-and-white and colored, have passed by—more or less imperfect reproductions of immortal works. Deep, infallible belief in divine rule and longing for salvation are evident in all these creations.

Significantly, I placed at the beginning of the book a bronze bust, wrought under the snow-covered glory of the Himmalayas which gives convincing expression to the thought of salvation: Bodhisatva Padmapani (Tibetan: Dschen-re-zee), son of Buddha Amitabha, had made a vow to redeem all creatures, man and beast, forever. Because he was not able to do so, he despaired and in grief his head split into a thousand pieces. His noble father, full of pity and mercy, formed ten new heads out of the fragments which he set on his beloved son in the form of a pyramid. As a crown he added his own head. Often, sitting at my writing desk I look up at him when the written word seems too paltry, unworthy of the noble subject. Then a solemn stillness comes over me, and out of the deep absorption of the benevolent face, new courage and strength flow into me.

The book leads the reader to sixty-nine places of note. They are spread over an area that is six times as large as the German-speaking territories in the heart of Europe. Enchanted, we look from mountain tops from which whole temple cities extend to hot, sunbaked plains, over which hover the ghosts of a glorious past. With hesitating steps we roam through desolate jungle towns, where fever broods, and dreary steppes, where the tiger still lies in wait. Not the India of the international tourist stream around the diplomatic quarter of New Delhi, the Taj Mahal Hôtel in Bombay, and the Taj Mahal in Agra, nor the modern India of dams, hydroelectric power stations and mills, schools, factories and hospitals which the leaders of the young Indian Union prefer to produce—with justified pride in the achievements of only a few years. No, a quite different India, which, as the author continually discovers, is fully unknown to a great number of the most educated of its own people.

Asoka, the great Buddhist Emperor, who is separated by only half a century from the Macedonian king, Alexander, and Charles V's famous contemporary, Akbar the Great, "King of Kings," "the Shadow of God!". Mighty rulers rise from their tombs and also out of the mysterious depths of ancient rock monasteries. Over the space of two thousand years rings the glad message of the Exalted One, the king's son from Kapilavastu at the foot of the Himalayas, who left his temporal kingdom in order to become ruler in the kingdom of the spirit and to plant a tree in the park of Sarnath, under whose shady, wide-spread branches milliards of men have found refreshment. Pagan, Vijayanagar, Mandu—all these kingdoms with their large cities, whose ruins the reader may have admired in silent respect and perhaps a little ashamedly—all these giant empires of Buddhist, Hindu or Moslem kings and emperors—they came and went. Only the kingdom of Buddha, "the Enlightened," remained; for it was not of this world.

Tree-shaded, crudely hewn snake stones, evidence of ancient superstition and demon worship, and juxtaposed, Jakanacharya's magic edifices, in which religious fervor and artistic creation achieved the highest spiritualization. Temples dreaming on mountain tops, near to the clouds, and to heaven, temples dreaming in maritime solitude, encircled by feathered palms and breaking waves that eternally return—*Eternal India!*

Governments come and go, nations change and lose their faces. India too is in the midst of exciting transformation. Among the messengers who travel up and down the country in the subcontinent between Cap Cormorin and Kashmir, bringing salutary messages and economic cures with them, there are many who bring stones instead of the promised bread. Swiftly and thoughtlessly they loosen thousand-year-old religious and family ties—under the much mis-used slogan "freedom." But they uproot the Indian; they make him not free, but restless, and take his best from him. Dam and tractor are an indispensable necessity to the Indian peasant, who must feed four hundred millions from a soil that is anything but that of a tropical paradise. Refrigerators, cinemas, air conditioners are also the dream of the modern Indian town-dweller, whom the Moloch of Industry has enticed away from his village plot, from his great family unit that offered him protection and refuge in every phase of life, and who crowds more and more into the large, hot cities with their insoluble social problems and dangers.

Will India, too, pay for the blessings of the West—the real and the supposed ones—with its life blood, with its own soul? Apprehensively and a little sadly, I gaze into the clouded flow of the motherly river, that eight years ago took to herself the mortal remains of the great Ghandi. With prophetic clarity the Mahatma recognized the internal dangers which loomed ahead for his homeland, now free from external compulsion. May India remain true to his spiritual legacy and dutiful example!

All those who recommend to the Indian, the American or some another imported way of life unnatural to him—often with suspicious zeal and deafening volume—forget or do not under-stand that machines, which they themselves in vast overestimation of technical achievement regard as inspired, really murder man's soul and that skyscrapers obscure the view of the sky.

India has blessed mankind with creative achievements, of which no other land in the world, the old or the new, was capable. Therefore, at the conclusion of my book, I call upon my reform-zealous friends, especially the younger ones among them, with the entreaty:

> Do not forget the best—
> "The profound thought of your sages,
> The serene light of your Art!"

Written on the eighth anniversary of the death of Mahatma Ghandi, (January 30, 1956) at Banaras, by the waters of the sacred Gangas.

A. N.

TABLE OF DATES

The table contains only dates that bear some relation to the contents of this book. Although the most reliable historical sources were employed, small chronological inconsistencies are unavoidable owing to the legendary character of much ancient tradition and by the many different calendars and chronologies used in India; the manifold Indian alphabets, languages and dialects account for variations in the spelling of Indian proper names.

3000 B.C.: Height of the pre-Aryan "Indus" civilization reaching back to the fourth millenium (Harappa, Mohenjodaro).

2000—900 B.C.: Aryans settle in North India.

1200—1000 B.C.: Pre-Homeric times, origin of Hymns of Rigveda (according to other research the Songs of Rigveda date five hundred years earlier).

624 B.C. (according to the canon of the Indian Mahabodhi Society): Birth of Siddhartha Gautama (Buddha) at Kapilavastu in Nepalese Himalaya. 544 his entry into Nirvana (in Kasia-Kusinagara).

599 B.C.: Birth of Vardhamana (later called Mahavira, "great hero"), founder of the Jain brotherhood, north of Patna, the ancient Pataliputra, also in North India. Like his contemporary Buddha, he comes from the caste of the Kshatriyas, warriors and political leaders.

6th or 5th century B.C.: Origin of the Ramayana epic, allegedly by Valmiki, often to be found on temple friezes.

518 B.C.: The Persian king Darius visits Punjab and Sind, most eastern Satraps of his Empire.

326 B.C.: Alexander the Great in Northwest India where King Paurava (Porus) offers bitter resistance on the Jhelum river.

262 B.C.: Emperor Asoka (274—232) of Maurya dynasty, ruler of Magadha, converted to the reform doctrines of Buddha, which becomes state religion. The Emperor visits Sravana Belgola and sends messengers to China. His son (or brother?) Mahinda (Mahendra) introduces Buddhism into Ceylon where Dewanampiya Tissa is king (307—267).

4th century B.C.—729 A.D.: Anuradhapura becomes capital of Ceylon. It covers an area of 256 square miles and achieves greatest splendor in first decades of first century.

2nd and 3rd century A.D. (Manu's codex): Already sharply determined caste system with inheritance of profession: the Brahmins, Kshatriyas, and Vaisyas opposed to the probably non-Aryan Sudras, are the four chief castes. Under the Kushan kings who ruled over Northwest India in the first two centuries, flourish the schools of Art in Mathura and Gandhara.

4th century A.D.: Gradual renaissance of Brahminism.

401—440 A.D.: Visit of Chinese pilgrim Fa Hsiën to the sacred places of Buddhism in North India.

5th century A.D.: Mahanama, a scholarly monk of royal blood, writes the Mahawansa, the famous, legend-interwoven Chronicle of Singhalese Kings, on leaves of the Talipot palm in Pali, sacred language of Buddhism.

300—600 A.D.: In North India the Imperial dynasty of Guptas, under whom the Arts flourish (Dhamekh Stupa of Sarnath; Kalidasa composes the Sakuntala).

c. 500 A.D. (time of Ostrogoth king Theoderic the Great, who lived on in saga as "Dietrich von Bern"): 18-year-interregnum while Kasyapas I was on the rock fortress Sigiriya, after the murder of his father. Genesis of the Sigiriya frescos, which far surpass the Ajanta murals through five centuries.

550—753 A.D.: Chalukyas (Badami) rule in South India.

6th century A.D.: Syrian (Nestorian) Christians in Travancore and Cochin (a small Jewish colony on the Malabar coast already in third and fourth centuries A.D.).

570 A.D., August 29: Birth of Mohammed in Mecca.

622 A.D., July 16: His flight to Medinat-un-Nabi (Medina). Beginning of the Mohammedan calendar.

629—645 A.D.: The Chinese scholar Hiuën Tsang travels through India in reign of the tolerant king Harsha, who also rules Nepal.

7th century A.D.: Rule of Pallava kings in South Deccan, who created the magnificent rock sculpture, and monolithic temple of Mahabalipuram, south of Madras.

Mid-7th century A.D.: Brahminism has regained its former significance (Elephanta); Buddhism departs from the land of its birth.

711 A.D.: In the same year as the Arab general Tarik destroys the Visigothic Empire at Xerez in Spain, the Moslems invade North India; conquest of Sind.

725—755 A.D.: King Dantidurga of the Rashtrakuta dynasty that ruled until the end of the tenth century, builds Kailasa temple at Ellora, the greatest monument of Hindu art.

735 A.D.: After destruction of the Sassanide Empire by the Muslims, the first Parsis (Zoroaster's followers) settle in India.

8th century A.D.: Although India has to defend herself against the violent attack of Islam, Indian art and culture are strong enough to conquer peaceably ever greater territories in Southeast Asia (Thailand, Cambodja, Indonesia). In the second half of the eigth century Buddhism conquers the whole of Tibet by peaceful means.

1000—1300 A.D.: Height of Indian temple architecture: Belur and Halebid, Dilwara temples on Mount Abu; Bhubaneswar in Orissa and Khajuraho in Bundelkhand.

1044—1077 A.D.: Rule of King Anawrata, comparable with Asoka, over great parts of Burma from Pagan.

c. 1135 A.D.: Jakanacharya, next to the unknown craftsman of Ranapur, the most outstanding artistic personality in India, was building the temples of Belur, Halebid, Somnathpur, in the service of the Hoysala kings.

From 1153 (or 1164?) A.D.: The Great Parakrama Bahu I of Polonnaruwa ruled over Ceylon for 33 prosperous years. Polonnaruwa has been the capital since 781.

1287 A.D.: Pagan becomes subject to China.

1295—1316 A.D.: Ala-ud-din Khilji resides in Delhi. He was conqueror of the Malwa kingdom, and destroyer of Sidhpur in the second year of his reign.

End of 13th century A.D.: Upper Burma invaded by the armies of Kubla Khan.

1298 A.D.: Marco Polo in India on return journey from China.

1309 A.D.: Malik Kafur, commander of Ala-ud-din Khilji's, conquers Warangal, and Halebid one year later (executed 1316).

1326 A.D.: Halebid destroyed by brutal Muhammad ibn Tughlaq (1325—1351).

1336 A.D.: Foundation of Vijayanagar Empire that flourished until 1565 (Battle of Talikota).

1398 A.D.: Timur plunders Delhi.

1459—1511 A.D.: Mahmud Bigara king of Gujarat, that already came under the banner of the Prophet (Mohammed) in 725.

1469 A.D.: Birth of Nanak, founder and first Guru of Sikh community (died 1538).

1489—1686 A.D.: Rule of the builders, the Adil Shahi; sultans in Bijapur.

1498 A.D.: Vasco da Gama in Calicut (dies 1524 in Cochin).

1505 A.D.: Portuguese on coasts of Ceylon. Native kings transfer their residence to the practically inaccessible, high-lying Kandy, that remains capital till 1815.

1509—1530 A.D.: Krishnaraya Emperor of Vijayanagar.

1510 A.D.: Affonso d'Albuquerque takes Goa.

1512—1687 A.D.: The "wealthy" Golconda, residence of Kutb Shahis.

1530—1556 A.D.: Humayun Emperor of Delhi: 1535 storms the fortress of Champaner. Defeated by the Afghan Shah, flees in 1540 to deserts of Rajputana for fifteen years.

1542—1552 A.D.: Francis Xavier (born 1506) as missionary to India. Death in China; his grave in Old Goa. — Despite four hundred years missionary work the number of Indian Christians is only five million out of a population of 438 million, according to the last census in 1951. A less than modest result when one considers that the majority of converts are members of the lowest castes that accepted Christianity for material reasons.

Friday, 5. Rabi-us-sani 963 = February 19, 1556 A.D. (some Moslem historigraphs begin a new calendar here, the beginning of a new, glorious era for Islam and the history of India): Ascent of Humayun's son, the great Akbar, one of the most active and wisest rulers of all time and all nations, to the Mogul throne. He secures the strategically important Ajmer, conquers the Malwa kingdom in 1562 and Kashmir 1586. His place of birth in Umarkot, his tomb in Sikandra (the Philosopher-King died in 1605). Under Akbar and his successors the Persian-influenced, courtly miniature painting on ivory and parchment is developed to highest perfection (Ustad Mansor).

1565 A.D., January 23: The allied Deccan sultans utterly defeat the Hindus at Talikota on the classic battlefield between the Tunghabadra and Krishna (Kistna) rivers, which has already witnessed 28 battles between Hindus and Moslems: 2000 Hindu elephants face Islam artillery of 600 cannon and 750,000 Hindu warriors a disciplined Moslem force of 400,000. After the battle of Talikota, which in size of troops and calibre of the mortars, has not seen its equal until the two World Wars, the star of Vijayanagar slowly sets.

1592—1615 A.D.: Man Singh, Akbar's general, Rajah of Jaipur state.

1600 A.D., December 31: Queen Elizabeth granted a Charter to the "Honourable East India Company." Cromwell renews the Charter in 1657.

1605—1627 A.D.: Jahangir (his wife Nur Jahan).

1619—1707 A.D.: Aurangzib (Emperor since 1658). He conquered Bijapur (1686) and the kingdom of Golconda one year later. After Aurangzib's death the Mogul Empire, having attained its greatest compass, begins to decline.

1627—1658 A.D.: Shah Jahan (the last fifteen years of his reign coincide with the first regency of Louis XIV). He built the Taj Mahal in Agra the marble mausoleum so praised by all visitors to India, for his wife Mumtaz-i-Mahal, the "Chosen One of the Palace," (a niece of the Empress Nur Jahan). — Shah Jahan Shahab ud din, "Lord of the world," the "flame of the faith" began his reign by murdering his brothers, blinded his nephew, and having his three cousins strangled. He died in 1665 as a state prisoner, unthroned by his own son, Aurangzib.

1665 A.D.: Bombay, since 1534 in Portuguese hands, becomes British. The city, with a population of 150,000 in 1800, now as large as the kingdom of Norway.

1672 A.D.: French settle in Pondicherry, returned to India in 1954.

1688—1747 A.D.: Nadir Shah of Persia. 1739 plunders Delhi, magnificent capital of the Great Moguls. The famous peacock throne, enthusiastically described by the French jeweller, Jean Baptiste Tavernier, and the Koh-i-noor ("mountain of light") from Akbar's tomb in Sikandra, are taken to Persia as trophies.

1728—1744 A.D.: Jai Singh II, the royal astronomer and builder of five famous Indian observatories, resides in the newly founded capital of Jaipur.

1767—1799 A.D.: The four bloody Mysore wars. 1799 Tipu Sultan, Haidar Ali's son falls fighting heroically at the defense of the "Watergate" at Seringapatam.

1796 A.C.: Ceylon becomes British.

1808—1886 A.D.: James Fergusson, the "Winckelmann" of Indian history of art.

1829 A.D.: Ending of cremation of widows.

1838—1904 A.D.: Jamshedji Nusserwanji Tata, son of an Old-Parsis priestly family from Bombay, one of the most highly-gifted industrialists of all times, creator of an national Indian textile industry, pioneer in the modern industrial development of India.

1857 A.D.: The great Indian "Mutiny." After its bloody suppression, removal of the privileges of East India Company by proclamation of Queen and Empress Victoria.

1879—1881 A.D.: Construction of the Darjeeling—Himalaya railway: 51 miles long.

1879 A.D.: King Thibaw, fifth successor of Alaungpaya (Alompra) who had founded Rangoon in 1755, kills off in bestial fashion the majority of the royal family shortly after ascending the throne, and creates conditions that lead to the invasions by the English into Mandalay (November 28, 1885). On January 1, 1886 Upper Burma is incorporated into the Empire. (Thibaw, in the hideousness of his misdeeds comparable to Shah Jahan, ends his inglorious life in Indian exile in 1916. The horrors of the First World War had put him into oblivion.)

1911 A.D., December 12: "Coronation Durbar" in Delhi. King George V, accompanied by Queen Mary, is crowned as Emperor of India. By solemn proclamation the capital of India is restored from Calcutta to the old Mogul residence. In both World Wars England had most valuable support from India, which was represented at Versailles by the Maharaja Sir Ganga Singh of Bikaner, a prince of the ancient Rajputan family.

1933 A.D., April 3: First flight over the 29,002-feet high Mount Everest.

1947 A.D., August 15: Arbitrary division of Bengal, the Punjab and rupture of Indian subcontinent, leading to bloody excesses und unspeakable refugee misery. Pakistan is made into new state. According to the last census in 1951 this largest Mohammedan state with its capital, Karachi, has a population of 76 millions, of which 86 per cent profess to Islam, and more than 42 millions live in the enclave, East Pakistan (East Bengal).

1947 A.D., August 15: End of British rule over India, exactly ninety years after the Sepoy uprising, that shook English rule to its roots. (None of the great Indian princes, subject to England, took part in this first war of independence.)

1948 A.D., January 30: Gandhi, the "Father of the Nation" (b.1869) assassinated by a Hindu fanatic in Delhi.
February 4: Ceylon, until now a Crown colony, attains Dominion status.

1949 A.D., November: Legal suppression of the "Untouchability" with its personal defamation and all its degrading social disdain for more than 50 million Indians.

India's Flag: Three horizontal stripes (saffron, white and green) with the sacred wheel of Buddhism in the center.

State coat-of-arms and symbol of Indian Union is the capital of an edict column of the Emperor Asoka, which is preserved in Sarnath: four lions, seated back to back in a circle, of astounding verisimilitude, guard the Wheel of the Law, which the "Enlightened One" first put into practice at this sacred place.

LIST OF TOWNS

(See map at end of book)

B = Burma, C = Ceylon, P = Pakistan. The letters and figures in parenthesis indicate the location on the map.

Ahmadabad 21, 22, 89—92 *(C 4)*

Aiholi 56 *(D 5)*

Ajanta 83—85 *(D 4)*

Ajmer 97 *(D 3)*

Amarapura B 5 *(G 4)*

Amber (Jaipur) 94 *(D 3)*

Anuradhapura C 12, 13, 17 *(D 7)*

Aurangabad 70 *(D 5)*

Badami 54 *(D 5)*

Belur 48 *(D 6)*

Bijapur 67—69 *(D 5)*

BURMA 1—7

CEYLON 8—17

Champaner 86, 87 *(C 4)*

Chamundi Hill (Mysore) 34 *(D 6)*

Chidambaram 30 *(D 6)*

Dabhoi 88 *(C 4)*

Dwarka 98 *(C 4)*

Elephanta (Bombay) 72 *(C 5)*

Ellora 77—82 *(D 5)*

Girnar 107, 108 *(C 4)*

Gulbarga 71 *(D 5)*

Halebid 38, 44, 45 *(D 6)*

Hyderabad-Deccan 64, 65 *(D 5)*

Hyderabad-Sind 106 *(C 3)*

Jamnagar 93 *(C 4)*

Kalugumalai 24 *(D 7)*

Kandahar (Afghanistan) 105 *(B 2)*

Kanheri 76 *(C 5)*

Karli 73, 74 *(C 5)*

Karur-Distrikt 23, 27 *(D 6)*

Kheda 102 *(C 4)*

Kondane 75 *(C 5)*

Kumbakonam 29 *(D 6, 7)*

Lakkandi 49, 51 *(D 6)*

Madras 117 *(D 6)*

Madurai 19, 20, 25 *(D 7)*

Mamallapuram 31, 32, 40, 41 *(D 6)*

Mandalay B 7 *(G 4)*

Mandu 116 *(D 4)*

Mihintale C 8 *(E 7)*

Mohenjo Daro P 103 *(C 3)*

Moodhera 96, 99, 100 *(C 4)*

Mount Abu 104, 109 *(C 4)*

NEPAL: Frontispiece

Pagan B 2, 3 *(G 4)*

PAKISTAN 103, 106, 111, 112

Palampet 63 *(D 5)*

Palitana s. Satrunjaya

Pattadakal 46 *(D 5)*

Pegu B 4 *(G 5)*

Polonnaruwa C 9—11 *(E 7)*

Rameswaram 18 *(D 7)*

Ranapur 110, 115 *(C 3)*

Rangoon 1 *(G 5)*

Sagaing B 6 *(G 4)*

Satrunjaya 113 *(C 4)*

Seringapatam 36 *(D 6)*

Sidhpur 114 *(C 4)*

Sigiriya C 14—16 *(E 7)*

Sinnar 95 *(C 5)*

Somnathpur 37, 39 *(D 6)*

Sravana Belgola 42, 43 *(D 6)*

Sri Rangam 28 *(D 7)*

Tadpatri 62 *(D 6)*

Tanjore-Distrikt 117 *(D 7)*

Tatta P 111, 112 *(B 3)*

Tiruvannamalai 35 *(D 6)*

Trichinopoly 26 *(D 7)*

Vadnagar 101 *(C 4)*

Vellore 33 *(D 6)*

Vijayanagar 47, 50, 52, 53, 55, 58—61 *(D 6)*

Warangal 57, 66 *(D 5)*

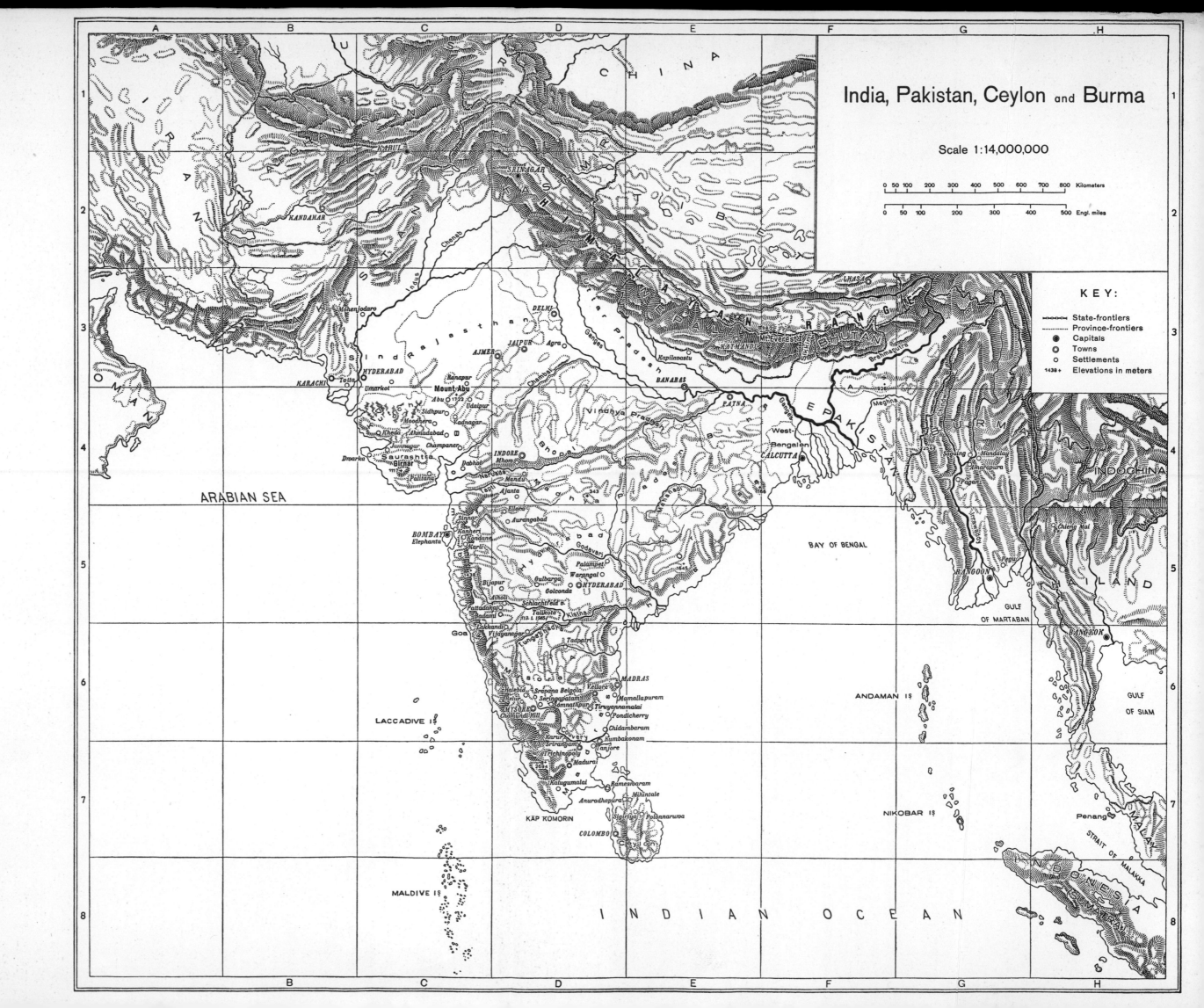

India, Pakistan, Ceylon and Burma

Scale 1:14,000,000

0 50 100 200 300 400 500 600 700 800 Kilometers

0 50 100 200 300 400 500 Engl. miles

KEY:
State-frontiers
Province-frontiers
● Capitals
◎ Towns
○ Settlements
1438+ Elevations in meters